The Gift to Listen, the Courage to Hear

THE GIFT TO LISTEN,
The Courage to Hear

~

CARI JACKSON

Augsburg Books
MINNEAPOLIS

To my mother, Gladys,
and to my father, Robert,
in memoriam, who showed me
the transforming power of love

~

THE GIFT TO LISTEN, THE COURAGE TO HEAR

Copyright © 2003 Augsburg Fortress. All rights reserved. Except for brief quotations in critical articles or reviews, no part of this book may be reproduced in any manner without prior written permission from the publisher. Write to: Permissions, Augsburg Fortress, Box 1209, Minneapolis, MN 55440.

Large-quantity purchases or custom editions of this book are available at a discount from the publisher. For more information, contact the sales department at Augsburg Fortress, Publishers, 1-800-328-4648, or write to: Sales Director, Augsburg Fortress, Publishers, P.O. Box 1209, Minneapolis, MN 55440-1209.

Cover and book design by Michelle L. N. Cook
Cover art from PhotoDisc

Library of Congress Cataloging-in-Publication Data
Jackson, Cari, 1956-
  The gift to listen, the courage to hear / Cari Jackson.
    p. cm.
  ISBN 0-8066-4552-0 (alk. paper)
  1. Listening—Religious aspects—Christianity. I. Title.
BV4647.L56 J33 2003
153.6'8—dc21   2002013202

The paper used in this publication meets the minimum requirements of American National Standard for Information Sciences—Permanence of Paper for Printed Library Materials, ANSI Z329.48-1984. ⊕ ™

Manufactured in the U.S.A.

07   06   05   04   03   1   2   3   4   5   6   7   8   9   10

CONTENTS

ACKNOWLEDGMENTS

To Linda David, Tina Jackson, Kelli Martin, Corinne Nelson, my family at the Riverside Church, my sister-scholars at Union Theological Seminary, focus group participants, clients, friends, and strangers whose comments about the value of this book kept inspiring me to write throughout five hectic years when it could have been easy to stop writing. Special thanks to Jewelle Gomez, who showed me how to craft more clear, yet colorful writing, and to Leslie Shiel, who helped awaken my poet's voice. Much appreciation to The Africana Literary Archives, which provided me (and other blossoming African American writers) with opportunities to connect with editors, agents, and publishers. To Steven E. Jones, Britton Jonathan Jackson, and Dr. Venus Green, blessings for providing me writing spaces that nurtured me at critical times. Thanks to Susan Blain and Malaika Adero, who critiqued and edited the manuscript in its different iterations and whose comments helped me sharpen my focus. Love and thanks to my sister-friend Robin Owens, whose spiritual support, friendship, and love sustained me throughout this process. Special thanks for the courage and vision of Michael Wilt and all of the Augsburg Books staff for believing in this project. Finally, I give thanks to the Spirit who gave me some insights about human relationships and then compelled me to write. What each of you has given to me is wrapped in every word of the pages that follow. Bless you.

INTRODUCTION

~

When we want to understand something, we cannot just stand outside and observe it. We have to enter deeply into it and be one with it in order to really understand.
    —Thich Nhat Hanh, *Peace Is Every Step*

Have you ever wondered why, despite your best efforts to help a friend solve a problem, the conversation ended with your friend feeling angry and you feeling frustrated? Have you ever used your best listening techniques and yet your spouse complained of feeling unheard? Have you ever taken a course of action, expending lots of money, time, or other resources based on what you heard clearly in a discussion, only to discover later that your actions were not what the other wanted or needed? If your answer to any of these questions is yes, you are not alone. If your answer is yes, this book can help you.

At first, I resisted writing this book because I did not want anyone to expect that I would be a *perfect* listener. The truth is, sometimes I am very good at listening and other times I am not. What helped me decide to proceed with this project is my passion for helping myself and many others improve our relationships. I am convinced that relationships—with spouses, children, parents, friends, coworkers, and so on—can become more respectful, loving, and nurturing when listening occurs from one's soul into the soul of another. When these relationships are strengthened, they provide the framework for transforming our homes, workplaces, communities, and even our world.

I have further been motivated to write this book at the urging of clients with whom I have used the principles and techniques outlined here. A few years ago, while doing consulting work in the areas of interpersonal communication, conflict management, and diversity education, I observed that most of the conflicts that arose

~

in organizations came about because colleagues in the workplace were not really listening to and hearing one another. They talked a lot, but listened very little. As a result, they either misinterpreted or did not hear at all what one another was saying. They often related to one another based on assumptions and fears fueled by misinterpretations and misunderstandings.

As I studied these interactions, I discovered three vital truths about human interaction. First, people need to feel safe in order for communication to work effectively. Second, in order to feel safe, people must feel heard. Third, as people feel safe, they become more respectful and loving and more willing to share the most treasured parts of themselves. People are more willing to take the risks needed for greater honesty and deeper intimacy in relationships when they feel safe. Competing with these truths, however, is the reality that most people do not know how to listen very well. As a consequence, human interaction often thwarts the safety needed to foster love and respect. Yet it would not serve us well to stop talking with each other. We need each other.

Given these competing realities, I asked the question, "What makes it so hard for people to listen?" I discovered three key factors. First, we learn to listen by what is modeled for us. Thus, if there is more talking than listening being done in our environment, we are likely to do the same. Second, we assume, based on our experiences, that people will not listen to us; many of us therefore spend a lot of time trying to ensure that we get heard, rather than listening. Third, our spiritual and emotional condition shape how we listen. If we feel broken, empty, depressed, or angry within our own spirits, we have limited energy for listening to others.

As a consequence, how we listen to one another often gets caught up in a cycle. Everybody talks, longing to be listened to and heard, but nobody is listening. Thus it is rare for anyone to get what we all want—the experience of being heard and knowing we are valued.

Most of us have been led to believe that speaking effectively is the most important aspect of communication. As a consequence, we have not focused much attention on learning to listen well. Yet the truth is that listening is as vital to communication as speaking. This is so because language is imprecise. No matter how hard we strive to create clear meanings when we speak, if others are not listening well, the meanings may not be received as we intend them.

Many of us use "active listening" techniques to help us understand what our conversation partners intend. Active listening techniques focus on the interpersonal transaction of communication—that is, the aspects of conversations that happen *between* two people. Active listening offers such techniques as restatements, observing body language, and framing speech in "I" statements to help sharpen the communication between individuals. In spite of our best efforts to employ such interpersonal listening techniques, communication often still goes awry. This is because listening involves more than interpersonal exchange. Listening is also an *"inner*-personal" activity. Effectiveness as a communicator begins within, by listening deeply to one's own soul. Listening is more than an aspect of communication; it is also a spiritual process.

To foster this kind of listening, I have developed what I call "soul listening" techniques. Soul listening enables listeners to go beyond the interpersonal focus of active listening to the inner-personal. Soul listening uses spiritually based listening tools that can enable you to connect more deeply with others by deepening your awareness of your own feelings. With greater clarity about your feelings, you can hear what others are saying more clearly.

This book interweaves listening techniques with spiritual principles that both undergird the importance of listening and provide a framework for how to listen more effectively. *The Gift to Listen, the Courage to Hear* is written in an easy-to-read, conversational style so that the information and skills needed to strengthen relationships can be readily implemented. I include a variety of stories to bring the concepts and techniques to life in practical ways. These stories are from my personal life, experiences with clients, and composites of conversations. Each chapter includes:
• real-life anecdotes to illustrate listening concepts
• spiritual principles that strengthen listening techniques
• practical tips for implementing listening techniques
• questions for daily reflection and practice to enhance listening

Part I explores the spiritual principles that undergird the important role listening plays in helping people grow into and express their grandest selves. Part II presents the most common causes of communication breakdown. And finally, part III offers specific strategies for moving to communication breakthroughs.

This book is designed for couples and singles, parents and adult children who are searching for ways to strengthen communication as a vehicle for building more harmonious and productive relationships within their families. It is a tool for work teams in business, religious, and community service organizations that are seeking more effective ways of working together. It is a teaching resource for professionals in social work, ministry, education, and other helping professions.

I have applied soul listening techniques in my personal life, my work with workshop participants, and consultations with clients and the results have been amazing. I trust and pray that these techniques will be useful for your homes, workplaces, and organizations. With this book and/or a journal, travel with me on a journey into your own soul, listening and learning all of the way. This is a journey of listening into wholeness. It will transform your relationships and your life.

Part I: The Holy Art of Listening

~

Holy listening—to "listen" another's soul into life,
into a condition of disclosure and discovery,
may be almost the greatest service that
any human being ever performs for another.
—Douglas Steere

~

ONE
THE SACRED ROLE OF LISTENING

~

"Hearing one another into speech."
—Nelle Morton, *The Journey Is Home*

Communication improvement programs have become big business in the past twenty years as individuals and corporations alike seek ways to be more efficient and effective. We attend workshops to learn better presentation skills. We seek to improve our letter-writing abilities and even improve upon our telephone and e-mail etiquette. We try to listen actively to our spouses and children, employees and clients. What guides much of our efforts is the belief that if we communicate well, we save a lot of time and resources and avoid heartache.

In addition to the important practical purposes of listening, there is a vital spiritual dimension that underlies why listening is so critical in all our relationships. That is, through listening we have the ability to help the speaker come to a deeper understanding of what is truly in his heart or on her mind, awaiting discovery. By listening, we can help others get clarity about their issues, which enables them to better express what they might not have had words for before. We have the capacity to bring another person's "soul into life" by listening.

The soul is the most essential aspect of the individual self. It is the core of the human being, the site of deepest clarity, insight, and wisdom. The soul is the site of the human being's encounter with and experience of the Divine, or God. By listening, we have the capacity to help others experience the presence and power of the Divine within.

Listening another person's "soul into life," to use Douglas Steere's phrase, is a holy and spiritual act. Each of us has the capacity for such listening, and we are called to such listening. It may seem

~

grandiose or exaggerated to claim that listening is holy activity. It may seem to be overspiritualizing a very common daily activity. Let me share with you why I refer to listening as holy activity.

Holy activity is any action, or even thought, intended to help people have greater awareness and experience of the divine life-giving power present in the universe. When we "listen another person's soul into life," we foster greater experience of the divine power within others and ourselves. Encounters with the holy *within* us often lead to transformation in our relationships with others and with the world around us, opening us to fuller participation in life-giving activities, such as fostering a sense of worth, safety, wholeness, and peace for individuals and communities. Our role as listeners is to help others create the emotional and spiritual conditions needed to discover and articulate the spiritual and emotional truths within their souls.

Listening at this level is soul listening, a spiritual process that simultaneously enables both listener and speaker to experience individual and collective divine wisdom more fully. Soul listening fosters the discovery of riches buried deeply within our souls. Discoveries of joy, power, peace, and liberty occur when we soul listen; that is, listen with our souls *into* the souls of others.

When we really make the time to soul listen and hear others, we send the message to them that they are important, loved, and valued by us. We foster within the speaker a sense of being valued for who she is. We help create a condition of safety in which the speaker can take the risk of opening to us her most prized possession—her soul. In opening her soul to the soul listener, she experiences the Divine Presence, God. When the Divine Presence is felt within the conversation, both the speaker and the listener are transformed. The speaker may find that fresh insight is available to her; new knowledge is manifest; clarity comes where there was only confusion; peace prevails where there had been discord.

Each of us can sense when another individual has developed the holy art of listening into the soul. The person who engages in soul listening lives with few self-protective walls of his own, he listens to and honors what he hears from his own soul, and demonstrates a great capacity for being emotionally and spiritually present to others.

The soul listener is able to break through the self-protective walls that others erect. He can gently breech the walls of aloofness, criticalness, overcontrol, cavalier attitudes, shyness, and arrogance to create an environment in which others may feel safe enough to be vulnerable. When your spouse, children, friends, colleagues, and even strangers sense the capacity within you to soul listen, they are much more likely to feel safe enough to explore, articulate, and share their grandest, divine selves.

LISTENING AS A SPIRITUAL PRACTICE

Some form or other of listening as a spiritual practice is encouraged to varying degrees by different spiritual traditions. For example, in Islam, the importance of listening to God the Creator is emphasized as the way to peace and well-being. In Judaism and Christianity, the wisdom of God is made available in human experience, but must be listened for, discerned, and interpreted carefully. In Zen Buddhism, the concept of listening deeply to others is stressed as part of right livelihood and living fully in each present moment. Taoist teachings center on listening to and surrendering to the Tao, which results in giving up judgments and desires and in becoming more compassionate.

Various texts that relate to the spiritual practice of listening are presented throughout this book. The sacred texts referenced in this book are used here framed by two beliefs:

1. as you listen from your soul to the souls of other human beings, you are listening to the Divine, and

2. as you strengthen your ability to listen to and honor the Divine voice within your soul, you become more able to listen to others.

LISTENING AS A SPIRITUAL SKILL

Soul listening is a spiritual skill that must be learned. Soul listening has nothing to with a physical ability to hear spoken words, but with the qualities of the heart, mind, and soul. It involves caring (the heart), intention (the mind), and courage (the soul). Soul listening is possible as you care enough about the quality of your relationships and your life to make changes in your approach, develop clear strategies for making changes, and have the courage to implement what you determine is needed. Soul listening does not focus on action outside of you, but within you, at your deepest level—your soul. Listening at this level does not come automatically. Soul listening is not part of a spiritual autonomic or involuntary reflexive process. It must be developed.

At first, using the skill of soul listening might feel somewhat awkward or it might require thinking about specific techniques and steps needed while engaging in it. Like any other skill, listening at the soul's level requires ongoing practice if it is to become second nature. The more we use it, the more proficient we can become. Without ongoing practice, we may not develop the degree of listening skill that may be needed in certain situations. Without practice, our emotional and spiritual ears may not be finely enough tuned to hear what is being said well below the surface. The more often we use the skill of soul listening in less emotionally charged situations, the greater our ability to listen well in emotionally volatile situations. We practice by listening to coworkers, loved ones, and strangers in low-key, everyday situations. We practice by listening to the sounds of silence. We practice when we listen to our heartbeats and our breath. We practice by listening to and getting in touch with what is being spoken within our own souls. Listening is a spiritual practice.

LISTENING TO THE DIVINE WITHIN

The Divine is within each living being. Often, caught in the busyness of our lives, many of us neglect to make spaces and times in which we can feel and encounter the Divine presence within us and within others. Making the conscious effort to soul listen to others also results in helping us experience stillness. Those moments of stillness, motivated by the desire to listen to another person, breathe life into us.

Divine activity and power are often experienced as whispers in the human soul. These whispers become more discernible through the stillness fostered by soul listening. Soul listening expands our ability to be perceptive at the emotional and spiritual levels. We become more able to hear the deeper activity occurring within our own souls and the souls of others. Each time we listen to another living being from the depths of our souls, we are listening to the Divine within others and ourselves.

NURTURING THE DIVINE WITHIN OTHERS

According to Buddhist monk Thich Nhat Hanh, when each person is born, she has within her the seeds of brilliance and beauty. Like flowers in a garden, she needs the right conditions—sun, water, fertilizer. When we engage in the holy activity of soul listening, we water the seeds of the Divine in others, enabling that which is divine within them to blossom and grow like a beautiful flower. Listening helps create the conditions for others to bloom.

Honoring the Divine within other human beings may awaken their awareness of the seed of the Divine within them. In order to soul listen, to be fully attentive—emotionally and spiritually—in our listening, we must set aside expectations about what others may say or think or feel or do. We must give attention in ways that say to others that we value them as a seed of God.

Conversations are like the precious buds that appear on a rosebush. Each time a new bud comes forth, it has the potential to either live or die. If the soil is conducive to new buds, they breakthrough into incredible beauty. As you listen, you can help cultivate healthy communication soil. The more you listen, the more conducive the soil becomes for fostering the growth of healthy connections. This is not to suggest that as a listener you have all of the responsibility for cultivating the kind of communication soil needed to keep conversations healthy and strong. Because both parties may take on the role of listeners at different times during the conversation, you and your conversation partner share in this responsibility. You do have certain responsibilities when it is your turn to listen. In some conversations that may be the bulk of your role, and not so in others.

The kind of listening being described here is effective because it does not remain solely at the surface level of the soil. The seeds of brilliance and beauty are planted deep in the soil of the soul. In order to nourish and nurture those seeds, the sun, water, fertilizer—all the conditions needed for growth—must have the capacity to go deep, beyond what can be seen on the surface. Soul listening enables the listener to hear not only what is being presented at the surface level but also to discern what is operating below the surface and to attend to those things in ways that provide the conditions for growth and healing. It is the listening we do below the surface that listens others into life.

During my years as a seminary student, I worked one summer as a hospital chaplain. Initially, I looked forward to the opportunity to share words of comfort with patients and their loved ones. I quickly learned that there are times when no words need to be spoken in order to be supportive and helpful to people who are facing extreme situations of life and death. In chaplaincy work, the act of listening to the spoken and unspoken words of patients is referred to as "the ministry of presence." There were times when there were no words for me to say, but for me to minister simply by being fully present emotionally and spiritually. What the patients needed most was for me to listen. They were not asking me to change or fix their circumstances, but to listen as they struggled in the midst of their circumstances. Sometimes they were silent, yet they still wanted me to listen. At times, they were saying good-bye to this life and wanted me to listen as a witness. Often it was in the times that I simply listened that patients or family members told me how much my visit meant to them.

One does not have to be trained and ordained as clergy to minister to others by presence. One *does* need the desire and the courage to feel and acknowledge others' personal feelings in ways that enable one to relate openly with them, while not overshadowing what they are experiencing.

Nurturing the Divine within You

In the process of helping to create the conditions that nurture others' souls into life, we, too, benefit. A greater sense of being alive is stirred in both the one being heard and the one listening. Like meditation, prayer, exercise, therapy, and other activities that help us become more attuned to psychic and spiritual energy, soul listening promotes emotional and spiritual health. Greater emotional and spiritual health begins with emotional and spiritual willingness to listen deep within oneself. Soul listening begins *within* each of us as we listen to our feelings and thoughts.

As my summer hospital chaplaincy progressed, and as I listened to and felt the stories of patients, I learned more about my own story as well. I learned that sometimes it was difficult for me to listen because their struggles caused me to face my own fears. Listening to patients demanded that I listen to, confront, and no longer be controlled by my fears. In working with patients I learned which illnesses I feared and what was behind this fear. Once I got this information about myself, I became freer. Once identified, those fears could no longer grip me. This was the gift I received as a direct result of listening to others from my soul. As I helped create the emotional and spiritual conditions in which others could feel safe to share from their souls, I was also nurtured by those conditions for health and growth in my own life in ways I could not have anticipated.

Soul listening to others enhances the spiritual and emotional conditions of our own lives. To strengthen your capacity to soul listen, consider the activities suggested below. Record your reflections in a journal or in the back of this book.

REFLECTION ACTIVITIES

1. Listen to your heartbeat and your breath at least six times each day for this week. Suggested times:
   a. when you awaken in the morning and before you get out of bed
   b. as you are preparing for your day's activities
   c. during your lunch
   d. while in a long conversation
   e. preparing for your dinner meal or other evening activities
   f. as you get into bed for the night.

What are your heartbeat and breath telling you about how you are feeling in each of those moments? Pay attention to any thoughts that you may be having in those moments.

2. During the next week, look for indicators in your behavior that signify when you are emotionally and spiritually available (that is, more able to be fully present to others) and when you are not. Availability might include: stopping what you are doing to listen to others, looking at people while they are talking, turning music down so that you can hear others, and so on. Unavailability might include: wondering when others will finish talking, thinking about things unrelated to the conversation, and so on.

3. Observe whether there are certain places, people, and times of the day, week, or month when you are more likely or less likely to be emotionally and spiritually available to listen.

4. What enhances your ability to be emotionally and spiritually available to others?

5. Think of a specific time when someone listened to you just the way you needed it most. How did that feel? What did that person do that helped you feel you really listened to and heard?

6. Think of a time that you were emotionally and spiritually ready to listen to someone. What did you do to help the other person know that you were ready and available?

7. Invite someone—your spouse or partner, your child, friend, parent, coworker, neighbor—to help you strengthen your ability to listen. Set aside ten minutes per day for one week to listen without offering advice unless requested.

    a. Ask your conversation partner to share any observations about your nonverbal behavior as you listened.

    b. As soon as possible after this ten-minute practice, jot down the thoughts and feelings that came to you while you were listening.

Two
The Universal Need to Be Heard

~

The lesson we must learn is that to love is to listen.
—Andrew Young, *A Way Out of No Way*

The need to feel heard runs so deeply within us that many people will share the most intimate details of their lives even with strangers. For example, observe the growth in television and radio talk shows where people have the opportunity to be heard by millions of strangers. Or notice travelers on a plane, train, or bus who often share deeply personal stories with fellow passengers willing to listen. Others, who when given a microphone at a meeting, will talk at length because they have been given the opportunity to be heard without interruption.

Throughout my childhood, my need to feel heard was greatly satisfied by my Gramas. By the time I was age four, I had adopted Gramas as my grandmother, for both of my grandmothers died before I was born. Gramas was a member of the church that my family attended, and she lived in the same apartment house as my family. Also, Gramas's married name was the same as my family name. So perhaps it was a matter of a shared destiny that I named Nancy Copeland Jackson as my Gramas. Because of Gramas's and my special connection, she became known as Gramas to my entire family.

Some of my favorite childhood memories are of times Gramas and I spent alone. I spent hours with Gramas learning about her world and sharing my childhood world with her. What made those times so special was that whatever was going on in her life, Gramas always made time and space to listen to me. Getting that attention from her made me feel loved and very special. My parents loved and nurtured me, yet with the demands of raising children, working, caring for older family members, and carrying out responsibilities in

~

our church and community, they often did not listen as much as I wanted or needed. The listening soul of Gramas nurtured me from childhood to adulthood. The gift of listening that Gramas gave me played a sacred role in my life. Her gifts of listening helped my soul blossom and thrive. As Gramas listened, I learned to speak. I was a very shy child in most circumstances, yet during my times with Gramas I experienced no shyness. I had full voice and articulateness when Gramas was listening. While it took years for this voice to be given expression in broader contexts, it was with Gramas that I first learned that I had something worth saying, worth being heard.

My story about Gramas is not just about a little girl who needed the listening attention of an older woman. It represents a need within every human being to feel heard at the deepest levels of the soul. Whether, and how, it is appropriate to satisfy this need may vary based on age, gender, culture, or other aspects of who we are and how we have been socialized. Yet the need is there within each of us.

LISTENING SENDS MESSAGES

When babies are learning to talk, everybody listens attentively. We do this whether or not we understand what the babies are saying. We often stop what we are saying and doing to listen to the novice speakers in our lives. In doing so, we send the message to them that they and what they are saying are valuable enough to deserve our full attention.

Unlike the young novice speakers, as children grow and develop their speaking skills they are given less attention by listeners who now take their speaking ability for granted. Thirsty for such attention, many of us resort to seeking it any way we can, even if not in very healthy ways. The earlier message of "Say anything you want, I am all ears" turns into "I don't have time to hear you now." For many speakers—whether children, teenagers, or adults—this translates to "You are not valuable enough for me to give you my attention right now." For children who cannot understand the concept of time as adults do, "right now" is the only time there is. So while the adults may intend to listen later, for children it means not being heard at all. Many children may interpret that to mean that they are not valuable.

The childhood experience of not feeling listened to stays in our minds and bodies as we grow into adulthood, even if the memories are not in our conscious thoughts. Every time we have an experience of not feeling heard, it aggravates those unhealed wounds from childhood. Even in situations where the other person has the best intentions to listen, we may nonetheless feel wounded and ignored.

For example, Tim was the youngest of three children. Because Tim was the first new baby in the family in eight years, he received a lot of attention. By the time he was age four, though, the excitement about him had settled down. Tim was much more quiet and reflective than his older siblings and his parents. As a consequence, during family conversations, Tim often did not have enough time and space to express his feelings. Because he was more introverted than his family members, Tim needed more time to reflect on and respond to the various issues discussed. Often by the time he finished processing his thoughts, the family was on to a new topic. When he did venture to share his thoughts, nobody really listened because they had moved on to something new. Tim often felt unheard. Throughout most of his growing up, he believed that what he had to say was not important. He did not expect people to be interested in listening to him. Tim's belief that his thoughts and feelings were not valuable has carried over into his adult life, particularly in his relationship with his wife. He is now reluctant to share his thoughts even when his wife pleads with him to do so. Because of patterns of the past, now Tim does not know how.

Hard to Speak Issues

Sometimes people struggle to share thoughts and feelings, not because of past experiences of feeling unheard, but because the issues they have in their souls are so emotionally loaded it is a strain for them to find the words. They are unable to articulate what is deep within them—a hope, trouble, or concern. Amidst this struggle, most people long to have someone's full, undivided listening attention to help them share and sort out their thoughts and feelings. In such moments, even greater tenderness is needed in the quality of the listening given. It is important for the soul listener to listen closely from the outset to gauge how emotionally and spiritually loaded the issue being presented may be. When we do not give our undivided attention in such times, we send the message that the issue is not that important and that the speaker's experience is not of value.

Several years ago, Lori, a young colleague of mine, came into my office to discuss something on her mind that was not work related. I listened to her while continuing my work. For years, I have been heralded as the "Multitask Queen," and as such, I felt that I could be an excellent listener *while* doing my work. Because I was responding to Lori with "yes," "um-hmm," and "really?" at the appropriate intervals in the conversation, I thought I was listening well. I was genuinely surprised when Lori said that she felt unheard and disrespected. My first thought was a defensive one: "After all, I am at work, and the things that she wants to talk with me about are not work related." Then I asked myself how I would feel if Lori engaged me the way I interacted with her. I knew that I, too, would feel disrespected. The fact that we were at work was an important, yet separate, issue. I realized that how I was listening was hurtful. I had sent Lori the message that neither she nor what she had to say were important enough for me to stop and look into her eyes and listen to her for even a minute. Lori was understandably hurt. I remembered how often I had experienced that same feeling as a child when my parents did not stop, look at me, and listen to me. I learned my multitasking-listening behavior from my parents. Without realizing it, I was acting in a way that had hurt me in my interaction with someone else.

I am not suggesting that every time someone wants to talk that we must stop everything we are doing and listen in order to help them know that we care about them and their issues. Whether at home or work, that is not always possible. But we do have choices.

By continuing to work, I was *indirectly* communicating to Lori that I was busy. Indirect communication is rarely good communication. In trying to do my work and listen simultaneously, I probably did neither well. I thought I was being respectful and emotionally present by making myself available to her even while I was working. But my half-listening did not feel respectful or satisfying to Lori. I had the respectful options of saying how much time I had available right then or asking if we could schedule a time so that I could give her my full, soul-listening attention.

After my conversation with Lori revealed how much my multi-tasking offended her, I began to notice how much this behavior affected others in my life. I learned that when I was on the phone, the caller could tell when I was working, watching television, reading, and so on. I had been doing this for years and had assumed that because no one had complained that they did not know or were not bothered that I was multitasking. Once my awareness was opened up to the possibility that a message of disrespect could be sent by my half-listening actions, it seemed that everything in the universe began to reinforce the notion that other people deserved more respectful attention than I often gave. Although my intention was to be helpful by listening, the *way* I listened was often hurtful.

For many of us, when we sense that a loved one or work colleague wants to discuss an important issue, we try to give focused attention. Most times, however, we cannot know what significance a particular issue may have inside someone else. Often, others want to test the communication ground with us to assess how safe it is for them to share what is on their hearts and minds. The extent to which we give respectful, focused attention largely determines how safe they feel with us.

At times, the other person may not even know himself how significant the issue is until he begins to talk or feels blocked from talking. Depending on how intertwined the issue is at the core of his soul, he may need a lot of skillfully gentle listening from you to help uncover what he is feeling and thinking. If an issue is intimately intertwined with a person's deepest longings or fears, it may be difficult for him to articulate them. When the speaker does not know what he really wants to say, soul listening is a way of helping him identify and articulate what he is thinking, feeling, or needing.

Many of us make the mistake of trying to intuit or sense what our loved ones, colleagues, or clients need in a given moment. Attempting to intuit other people's feelings is risky, and may lead to misreadings that result in frustration and hurt. Loving or respecting someone does not require that you be able to intuit what they are feeling or needing. Respect requires that you set aside your assumptions and your agenda regarding the needs of the other person, and that you open your heart to be emotionally and spiritually present with them. Soul listening in this way is an expression of the love and respect for which every human being longs.

As the listener, when you open yourself to the guidance of the Divine speaking deeply within your own soul, rather than trying to intuit what the speaker is seeking to express, you become much more able to help the other find her voice. As this happens, new and deeper knowledge can be accessed by the speaker, which benefits both participants in the relationship. Soul listening helps create the safety the speaker needs to uncover and express her deepest thoughts and feelings.

REFLECTION ACTIVITIES

1. Think of a person who you generally feel listens to and hears you. List specific things he or she does (behaviors, actions) that work best in helping you feel listened to and heard.

2. What have you thought, said, and done when you have felt ignored at a time you had a major issue you needed to discuss? What impact has that experience had on your ability to share your most emotionally intimate issues with others?

3. Observe your body language over the next week to learn more about what messages you may be sending to people as you are listening. Pay attention to:
   a. how much eye contact you give, the direction your body is facing in relation to the person to whom you are listening, and what else you may be doing while listening
   b. whether there are distinctions in how you listen face-to-face versus over the phone
   c. any distinctions in how you listen at work versus at home.

4. Observe your body language when you are listening and when you are speaking. What differences do you notice? What do these differences suggest to you?

5. Who are the people in your life who may need more of your full, undivided attention? List the things that you can do to fulfill that need.

6. When these individuals want your full listening attention and you are not able to give it, what can you do to demonstrate your love and respect for them, balancing their needs with your needs?

THREE
LISTENING TO AND LEARNING FROM FEELINGS

~

Music or the smell of good cooking
may make people stop and enjoy.
But the words that point to Tao
seem monotonous and without flavor. . . .
When you listen for it, there is nothing to hear.
When you use it, it is inexhaustible.
      —*Tao Te Ching*, No. 35

Honoring the feelings of the person speaking is the most important aspect of the holy art of listening. Honoring the feelings of others helps them not just be heard but also *feel* heard. While there are no magical listening techniques that are universally effective, there are some simple things that you can do in your listening that will help most people feel listened to and heard. The first of these is listening to and learning from your own feelings. This is where soul listening begins.

The more you are able to listen, honor, and understand your own feelings, the more you are able to listen and relate to the feelings of others. When connections are made at this level, you and others feel safe enough to engage in deep, mutual disclosure opening the path to rich discoveries from person to person, from soul to soul. You become more able to recognize the Divine within you and within others.

Recall a time when you really needed to tell somebody—spouse, parent, child, boss, or friend—about the upsetting and confusing events of your day, but your loved one had such a rough day himself that he needed to tell you about his struggles and was not available to hear about your day. Or remember a time that you confided in

~

your mother about a major decision you were making, but received advice that was not applicable, indicating a lack of attention on her part. Remember a time you talked with your boss, trying to prevent a recurring problem at work, only to see it happen again because your boss had not truly heard what you had said. Once again your boss was so busy assuming what you were going to say that she was not hearing what you actually said.

How did you feel when you experienced these conversations? sad? angry? frustrated? disappointed? Many of us try to "think away" such feelings by justifying why the other person was not able to listen or by rationalizing that "it wasn't that bad. She was trying to listen, but she had such a rough day herself." Or maybe saying, "I know he meant well. I should have been more direct about what I was needing—not his help in fixing anything, just for him to listen."

Often many of us have these experiences in which our need to be heard goes unfilled. We feel a sense of longing that we do not know what to do with or how to handle. Many of us deny or repress the feeling so we won't feel hurt by or angry with those we love or with those we need to work everyday. Whether we stuff down or deny the feelings of hurt or anger, the feelings are still there in our subconscious minds and in our bodies. There are consequences to stuffing these feelings—consequences to our individual well-being and our relationships.

SUPPRESSED FEELINGS

We prefer not to feel feelings like sadness, hurt, anger, loneliness, disappointment, and fear, so we deny, stuff, or ignore these feelings. Most of us refer to such feelings as negative feelings. We have been taught by our families, schools, and religious communities to believe that "ladies don't get angry," "men don't cry," and any number of other things about what and how we should feel. While the intentions of these messages were to help children navigate through life, they put limitations on our experiences of being fully human.

When feelings of anger or hurt are denied or suppressed, they do not go away. Instead they are held unconsciously and grow inside you every time you experience another hurtful or anger-provoking situation—whether in connection with the same person or someone else. Feelings that you are unaware of can become like noisy static in your listening systems. Despite your conscious efforts to attune yourself to listen to others, suppressed or denied feelings can create an emotional clamor inside your soul that impedes you from really hearing. Suppressed or denied feelings create emotional distance between you and others, often to the point that you neither have interest in talking with nor listening to them. When feelings are not expressed, relationships gradually die and no one knows when or why the death happened.

There are also consequences to your individual well-being. In particular, you may be more likely to minimize the value of your feelings, lose touch with your own feelings, and develop a fear of intimacy with people.

Your emotions, thoughts, aspirations, and accomplishments are extensions of your personhood. If any of these extensions of your personhood feels devalued by others, it feels like *you* are being dismissed and devalued. For example, you have just shared with your spouse how hurt you are about something that occurred at work and his response was "Honey, there is nothing to be upset about. Let it alone." Hearing these words hit you even harder and hurt you even more than the situation at work. This is because your very personhood feels dismissed and devalued. The fact that the injury occurs by the words of a loved one hurts even more deeply. Even if you minimize the value of your own feelings, the results are the same; that is, your personhood feels belittled.

Perhaps you have suppressed your feelings for so long that you are afraid of the possible consequences of expressing your anger or frustration. People have told me they believe that if they really let themselves release their tears they fear that they would never stop crying. Others have said that if they allow themselves to express the fullness of their anger they fear that they would experience such incredible rage that they would hurt someone. Many of us fear that we will lose control—that is, control of our well-trained emotions. The thought of that overwhelms many of us and causes us to continue stuffing down and denying our feelings.

For most of us, our concern about these possible consequences is a good sign that we are not likely to strike out uncontrollably in harmful ways. Generally, having a conscious recognition of the intensity of our feelings provides a helpful framework for handling the feelings. When we are disconnected from the feelings we are more likely to act them out in uncontrollable and inappropriate ways.

Expressing your feelings is part of the skill of listening. Use your feelings to help strengthen your soul listening skills by listening to and expressing feelings about issues that are not as deeply connected with your core identity. Allow yourself to be with those feelings. Experiment, initially, with ways to express uncomfortable feelings while retaining a measure of control, and gradually taper off the control mechanisms. For example, when you are alone in a wooded area or in your car (but not while driving), let yourself recall an unpleasant experience that still pains you and let yourself yell, scream, or cry. Give yourself a specific time limit for how long you will be fully in your feelings. At the end of the time, let your final thoughts be of a special heart-warming experience. Value and find healthy ways to express all of the feelings you have. Your feelings are expressions of your humanity.

LOSE TOUCH WITH ONE FEELING, LOSE TOUCH WITH ALL FEELINGS

Losing touch with a range of feelings is another unfortunate consequence of denying or suppressing feelings. Feelings can be suppressed to the point where you no longer recognize them when you experience them. Or maybe you still feel these feelings, but have forgotten or never learned how to express them in healthy, loving, effective ways. These emotions are what M. Scott Peck, in *The Road Less Traveled*, calls "uncomfortable" feelings. Peck points out that these feelings are not negative or bad in themselves. Rather, these feelings express our discomfort with some aspect of our experience. They give us important information about our emotional response to something we are going through.

If you constantly ignore or deny your uncomfortable feelings, you begin to lose touch with *all* of your feelings, including the pleasant ones. Despite what many of us want to believe, there is no way to block out only the uncomfortable feelings while continuing to fully experience the feelings we like. When you close the window to shut out the summer rain, in the process you also shut out the cool breeze after a hot, humid day. When you lose touch with or block out the uncomfortable feelings, you also minimize your ability to be in touch with your joys. You become emotionally numb.

Being in touch with all of your feelings is vital to healthy communication for four reasons: 1) it enhances your ability to engage others with language appropriate to their need; 2) it provides signs and markers to guide you through rough conversations; 3) it keeps you from absorbing other people's feelings; and 4) it minimizes the likelihood of projecting your feelings onto others.

LISTENING BILINGUALLY:
LEARN THE LANGUAGE OF FEELINGS

Being in touch with your feelings enhances your ability to relate with the feelings others have as you are listening to them. When one person is speaking from an emotional or feeling place and the other is relating from an intellectual or thinking place, it is hard to make an interpersonal connection. I have witnessed many conversations between people in which the frustrations for both parties mounted and mounted, not because they were not trying to listen but because they did not know how to listen the way the other person needed, that is, listen with their feelings.

For example, in a time of financial struggle in their business, Ron told his friend and business partner Emil about his anger and disappointment at not getting a new business contract. Ron expressed his confusion and frustration that after all of his hard work to develop a strong proposal he was still unsuccessful in getting the contract. Emil, who was out of touch with his feelings of fear, listened with and responded from his intellectual self, and suggested strategies to Ron about ways he could have improved his chances of getting the contract. As this continued, Ron grew more and more frustrated because his feelings were not being heard and he felt that Emil was putting all the blame on Ron for not getting the contract. Maybe this was the case, but Ron did not need to hear that right then. Emil was frustrated as well, because he was trying so hard to listen and help Ron and he didn't understand why Ron was becoming angry. The more emotionally Ron expressed himself, the more intellectually Emil related with him. Because Emil was not in touch with his own feelings, it made it difficult for him to understand and relate with Ron's feelings.

When two people are using the same cultural language— English, Korean, German, Spanish, Ebonics, what have you—we assume they have enough common ground to be able to communicate effectively. But this is not necessarily the case. There is also an interpersonal language being spoken, that of the intellect or feelings. Ron and Emil were speaking two different interpersonal languages— Ron, the language of feelings, and Emil, the language of intellect. Neither language is better than the other, rather they are simply two distinct languages. For healthy and productive communication, it is important to learn to be bilingual—that is, able to speak the interpersonal languages of both feelings and intellect—and to know when to use which one.

There are a few ways to distinguish feeling-based language from intellect-based language. Like Ron in the story above, when most people are using the interpersonal language of feelings, they use feeling words such as *angry, confused, disappointed, sad, hurt, glad, happy, thrilled*. Sometimes, however, feelings may be expressed in words that appear to be intellect-based. For example, in the statement "I don't know what to do," the word *know* appears to be intellectually based, but it may more accurately be a reflection of the emotion of fear that accompanies confusion and uncertainty.

Intellect-based interpersonal language is often characterized by efforts to explain and understand experiences, give advice, solve problems, and rationalize experience. Typical words and phrases used in intellect-based interpersonal language include *understand, clear picture, what you/we need to do, what is the plan?, what do you mean?*

Emil, in his efforts to support Ron, began giving advice and rationalizing what happened with Ron's unsuccessful contract bid. Ron, however, was not ready to think; he needed some time and space just to feel. Emil's intellectual strategy of dealing with defeat or disappointment is to think of ways to ensure that disappointment is less likely to occur again. Because they were speaking two different interpersonal languages, both men became frustrated that they could not communicate more successfully. Neither felt heard.

POINTING THE WAY TO UNDERSTANDING

Knowing your own feelings can help you navigate the seas of your conversations. Even when you are out of touch with your feelings, they have an unconscious impact on your communication. Unconscious feelings influence what you say as well as when and how you say it. And they influence your role as a listener, how you receive and interpret what you hear from others. When you know what you are feeling, you can make conscious choices about how you listen and how you interpret what you hear. When you know what you are feeling, you can assess more easily if your response to the other person is about what he or she is saying or more about some feelings you may have.

Here is an example. Peter and his fiancée, Christie, had a very emotionally loaded conversation about their relationship. During this conversation, Peter decided to end their engagement. He made this decision because Christie told him that she felt left out of his life when he made decisions that affected her, but did so without consulting her. She explained that every time Peter did this it made her wonder if he was really ready to get married. Hearing this, Peter decided that Christie was using this lame reason as an excuse not to marry him. Peter told her that perhaps it was best that they break the engagement. Christie and Peter love one another and want to be married. Neither of them understood what happened.

Let's look at what went on inside each of them. Peter thought he was making this choice to end the engagement based on what seemed to be a reasonable conclusion: Christie did not want to marry him. In fact, Peter's decision was based on his fear of being "dumped" by Christie. It was never in Christie's mind to end the relationship, but to share her feelings with Peter so that they could work on the issue together and strengthen their relationship. Because Peter was not in touch with his fear of being dumped—abandoned—by Christie, he could not hear what Christie was really saying to him. He made choices based on his fears instead of the real issues between him and Christie.

SEPARATING YOUR FEELINGS FROM OTHERS' PROBLEMS

Being in touch with your feelings helps you distinguish your own emotions from those of the people with whom you are relating. It helps you avoid the tendency to absorb their issues or project yours onto them. When your feelings become indistinguishable from those of others, your choices are likely to be based on issues and feelings not solely your own, and are therefore likely to be inappropriate to meeting your needs.

Ling experienced this difficulty in a conversation with her best friend Maria. Ling sought advice about how to handle some discomfort in her relationship with her boyfriend, Keith. In the course of the conversation, Ling realized that Maria was doing most of the talking. Maria was passionate about her feeling that Keith did not appreciate Ling and that Ling deserved better. Before she knew it, Ling was saying, "Yes, I do deserve better!" and began to think that she should break up with Keith. Later that same night, though, Ling asked herself why she had not recognized, before talking with Maria, the severity of her problem with Keith. As she continued to think about it, she realized that she was not as angry with him as Maria was. Ling began to recognize that some of the anger she was feeling was not solely her anger, but Maria's, and that Maria's anger was related to a series of unsuccessful relationships with men in her own life. Maria's anger bled into her listening style and brought confusion, rather than help, to Ling. Because Ling was unsure of her feelings for Keith, she easily absorbed Maria's feelings and incorporated them into her own.

When you are not well-tuned into your own feelings, it becomes easy to take on the feelings of other people, and even to believe those feelings are your own. If you are not careful, you may take actions based on what you *think* you feel, only to regret the actions later. Feelings are so fluid, and at times contagious, so take care to distinguish yours from those with whom you communicate.

AVOIDING PROJECTION OF YOUR FEELINGS

If you are not able to distinguish your feelings from those of others, you may be like Maria, who imposed her feelings onto Ling. You may intend to listen and support your loved ones, yet you begin to focus on your experiences and expectations, your hopes and history, and on your fantasies and fears instead of their concerns. You may impose or project your anger or fear onto others, all the while presuming that you really understand what *they* are feeling. You may think that you are really listening and being supportive, yet the one to whom you are listening does not feel heard or supported by you. Because you have *intended* to listen and be supportive, you don't understand why he does not feel heard, understood, and supported.

When you develop the skill of listening to and honoring your own feelings, you can more readily distinguish your feelings from others'. Your feelings can be important guides for relating with and understanding what others are saying to you from their·souls. The more practiced you are in this aspect of soul listening, the more attuned you will be to the hard-to-articulate messages of others.

REFLECTION ACTIVITIES

1. Like music, conversations are comprised of sounds and rhythms that reverberate at different levels.

    a. Listen to three different kinds of music—your favorite music, music you never listen to, and music you dislike. In your journal or in the back of this book, write down what you like and dislike about each genre of music, including information about how you felt during and after listening to each kind of music.

    b. After you have done this activity, listen to other people's conversations and identify what you like and dislike about their tones, pitches, paces, rhythms, volumes, word choices, body language. Write down your likes and dislikes and the feelings evoked from these conversations.

c. Compare your music and conversation lists. Identify the overlaps regarding the tonal quality, pace, rhythm, and volume. To what extent do these aspects of communication influence your feelings and thus, your ability to listen to others?

2. What messages did you learn in your home, school, and religious community about feelings of anger, sadness, fear, disappointment, and loneliness? What do you most often do when you experience these uncomfortable feelings?

3. How do you respond when the person you are listening to begins to express anger, sadness, fear, or other uncomfortable feelings? Of the following, which is/are your most likely response(s):
   a. encourage the person to share more about his or her feelings
   b. begin to have similar feelings
   c. begin to feel anxious
   d. wish the conversation would move on to something else
   e. try to solve the person's problem.
What do your responses suggest?

4. Think about a frustrating conversation in which it felt that you and the other person were speaking two different interpersonal languages. Which language was the other person using—emotional or intellectual? Which were you using? What was the outcome of the conversation?

5. Observe your conversations over the next week.
   a. Which interpersonal language do you use most often— intellectual or emotional?
   b. Based on the outcomes of the conversations, to what extent are you generally using the most effective interpersonal language to foster healthy and productive communication?
   c. To what extent are you able to vary between the languages of feeling and intellect depending upon your relationship with the other person?

Part II: Listening Killers

~

When you plant lettuce, if it does not grow well,
you don't blame the lettuce. You look into the reasons
it is not doing well. It may need fertilizer, or more water,
or less sun. You never blame the lettuce.
Yet if we have problems with our friends or family,
we blame the other person. But if we know how
to take care of them, they will grow well, like lettuce.
—**Thich Nhat Hanh,** *Peace Is Every Step*

~

Four
Lethal Listening Styles

~

The trouble with people is that they're busy fixing things they don't even understand. . . . It never strikes us that things [or people] don't need to be fixed. . . . They need to be understood.
    —Anthony de Mello, *The Way to Love*

The goal of communication is to enable people to understand each other and thus be able to live and work together effectively. Soul listening helps achieve this goal by enabling us to increase the self-understanding we need to listen more openly and freely to others. As we increase our self-understanding, we are more able to support the emotional and spiritual growth of others.

Understanding our own listening styles and the life issues that have shaped them is a vital aspect of soul listening. Just as each of us has different speaking and writing styles, we also have individual listening styles. When our general listening styles conflict with the speaking styles of others, communication is more likely to breakdown.

Following are ten common listening styles that often lead to disaster in conversations. I should know; I have used all of these lethal listening styles in my own life. The results have not been favorable, but based on my experience I can share with you listening behaviors to avoid and suggestions for more helpful behaviors to use. If there are listening styles listed below that you have not used already, do not try these at home or at work. I repeat: Do not try these at home, work, or anywhere. The consequences may be hazardous to your emotional and relational health.

~

THE ANALYST

Do you know anyone who always has a crystal-clear understanding of the underlying reasons for the problems in other people's lives? Someone who, instead of listening, is constantly analyzing everything other people say?

This listening style focuses on identifying and assessing the patterns, strengths, and weaknesses of the life choices that other people make. While these can be very useful skills to offer, they are rarely helpful when provided uninvited. For most people, the analyst feels like a judge who *evaluates* their lives and their choices. Even though it may not be the analyst's intention to criticize or judge, that is how the comments from this listener are generally received.

Here is an example. Joann and Stephanie have been coworkers and friends for two years. Stephanie has the highest respect for the strong analytical skills that Joann demonstrates at work. It was Joann's keen analysis that initially impressed Stephanie as they developed their friendship. Lately, however, it has really begun to irritate Stephanie when Joann insists upon analyzing why Stephanie has repeated the same unhealthy choices in her romantic relationships. Stephanie believes that what Joann says is probably very accurate, but sometimes she just wants Joann to listen and not try to analyze and figure things out in Stephanie's life. She did not ask Joann to be her therapist. Stephanie thinks that Joann has issues in her *own* life that she needs to focus on. Recently, Stephanie told Joann about a new person she was dating and immediately Joann began making references to the severe problems in Stephanie's previous relationship, warning Stephanie to be on guard against repetition of patterns from the previous relationship. Stephanie said, "I may make some bad decisions but at least I have the courage to date. Instead of analyzing my romantic relationships, why don't you analyze why you're too afraid to date at all?" In response, Joann asked, "Steph, what is all of this hostility about? I was only trying to help."

It is often more supportive to help others analyze and understand their own life choices and patterns than to do the analysis for them. The tendency to give your analysis signals the presence of issues within you to be explored. The *need* to share your analyses may be more for your benefit than for others. A super-sharp analysis that is motivated by a need to show how smart you are is not as helpful as one that is motivated by genuine love and concern. Also, a one-directional analysis that focuses on other people's lives is not as emotionally informed as analysis that extends to one's own life. The act of analyzing other people's situations can be used to avoid examining your own life more honestly. Often you may have such keen insight into other people's lives because something about their lives subconsciously resonates deeply within you about your own experience.

While some of us are more gifted in analyzing situations, everyone has some insights to offer. After toddler age, even children have insights that may be helpful to adults. But if you are the only one providing insightful nuggets, the relationship cannot grow. When you are the only person sharing analyses and insights, others do not feel valued and safe in the relationship. If your insights are the only ones being expressed, you may be speaking from your intellect when it is time to listen from your soul.

The Co-Optor

People generally take turns redirecting their conversations as part of the natural ebb and flow of communication. Redirecting becomes irritating, however, and can lead to a listening breakdown when it occurs in a nonreciprocal way, with only one person doing all or most of the rerouting. A co-optor redirects conversation topics so as to focus attention upon himself or a subject that matters more to him. Co-opting can be done so unobtrusively that it goes almost completely unnoticed, even by the person away from whom the focus was taken.

A conversation between Joseph and Traci demonstrates co-opting behavior. Joseph was trying to tell Traci about his recent vacation. Each time he shared a special experience from his trip, Traci would say, "Oh, that reminds me of the time I went to . . ." At first, Joseph did not notice this redirecting, but by the third or fourth time he started to get angry. When he mentioned this to Traci, she said that was her way of sharing in the conversation and letting Joseph know that she was really listening. But Joseph did not feel listened to at all. He felt that Traci, by dominating the conversation, was sending the message that she was not interested in hearing about his trip at all.

The rest of their time together, Joseph was very quiet and not very engaged in the conversation.

The tendency to co-opt a conversation is often motivated by one of two desires within the listener. First, the listener may desire to be listened to and receive undivided attention. Second, the conversation may be addressing an issue that evokes uncomfortable feelings in the listener, which he seeks to avoid by redirecting the discussion. In either case, redirecting indicates that the listener is neither aware of his own feelings nor attentive to the needs and feelings of his conversation partner.

THE DRIFTER

Comedian Ellen Degeneres includes in one of her routines a story about conversations with people who mentally drift away for sizeable periods of time. She can tell when people have drifted away by the glazed look that comes across their faces. Most of us have encountered people who drift away during a conversation. Many of us have been drifters. As listeners, we may drift away for any number of reasons that may or may not be related to the person speaking. Possible reasons include the monotone voice of the speaker, a topic that is not of personal interest, an emotional response triggered by the speaker or the topic, fatigue, preoccupation with something else, and so on. Of course, if you are the one speaking and your listener drifts away, it is hard *not* to take it personally. When someone drifts away, it is hard not to feel offended, even if what you are saying is not tremendously important to you. It hurts even worse if the topic is very close to your emotional bone.

Dwayne finally mustered the courage to talk with his wife Jessie about his interest in returning to college. Dwayne had dropped out of college in his junior year twenty years ago when Jessie became pregnant. Now that their children are in college, he's been thinking about completing his bachelor's degree and maybe going on to get a master's. Dwayne has always wanted to be an art teacher. As much as he wants to do it, he is very scared. Dwayne begins mentioning his thoughts to Jessie by saying, "Well, now that both our kids are in college, I might as well take my tired old self back to school before my brain cells all die out. I might become the next Picasso yet." Then Dwayne started reminiscing, telling funny stories from his college days. Because of the humor with which Dwayne mentioned his thoughts about college, Jessie did not know how important and scary it was for him. Dwayne's mention of their kids reminded Jessie of the care packages of goodies she planned to send to their daughters at college. Then she began thinking about what she needed to buy for the care packages and trying to figure out when she would have time to go to the store. As Dwayne realized that Jessie was not listening to him, he did not feel safe enough to share his fears about college with Jessie, so instead he changed the subject. As a consequence, Dwayne was not able to receive the encouragement and support that he longed for and that Jessie would have given him.

THE INTERRUPTER

What is regarded as interrupting is based on each person's cultural background or family experience. For example, in some cultures or families interrupting may suggest genuine interest in the topic being shared. In others, interrupting may be perceived as very rude. In general, however, and apart from cultural and family contexts, interrupting is not seen as a loving way to stay engaged and connected with someone. Interruptions may break the flow of the thoughts and feelings that the speaker is trying to share, and can result in the speaker having a conversation that feels as if she is walking on the deck of a boat in a very choppy sea. When it is hard to know where to place your feet solidly in a conversation, you may want to scream, "Let me out!" Interruptions can build anxiety and tear down trust.

In order to interrupt, you have to formulate your thoughts while the other person is still talking. Most of us are not as good as we want to believe we are at simultaneously listening to others and planning what we will say next. If you interrupt others often, it is a strong indicator that you may not be listening very closely. It is virtually impossible to listen from your soul into the soul of another person while interrupting. The depth of attention required by soul listening does not leave a lot of psychic energy for jumping to your next point.

Amy and Connie were spending their monthly Girls' Night Out together. This month, more than ever, Connie really needed this time. She was so tired from her daily activities of parenting, being a spouse, working, and so on. She had no deep intimacies she wanted to share, but just looked forward to a relaxing, stress-free time with Amy. Throughout the night, though, it seemed that every time she was telling Amy something Amy interrupted her in midsentence, midthought. At first Connie convinced herself that she was just tired and oversensitive. But it continued. Because they were good friends, Connie mentioned her feelings to Amy, and even while she was trying to explain what she was feeling, Amy interrupted her to explain that "It's never been an issue before. I haven't changed, maybe you have. Or maybe you're too tired to be out tonight." After that, Connie began thinking that next month, she would spend her Girls' Night Out by herself, afraid that spending that time with Amy would be too stressful.

The Interrogator

I have been in conversations with people who asked me such a battery of questions that I felt that either I was being interviewed by a relentless reporter of a less than reputable tabloid or was being interrogated under bright lights designed to make me confess even to things I did not do. Although the interrogator may be asking questions out of genuine interest, being asked many questions in rapid succession can make a person feel as if under attack.

Many of us come from families in which lots of things were kept private, and it does not feel very safe to be asked a lot of questions. We may have grown up hearing the adage "knowledge is power" and are afraid to let people have too much information about us—for fear of the ways they might use it. Following is an example of what the interrogator listening style might look like.

Isabella called her classmate Tim to bounce around some ideas she had about a school project. After the first few minutes of the conversation Isabella was ready to say good-bye because instead of having dialogue, she felt that she was being examined on a witness stand in a courtroom. Tim wanted to know everything that Isabella had done since their last conversation, three months earlier, because he had missed her. To Isabella, it seemed that Tim had a zillion questions, and all she was doing was responding to his questions instead of having a mutual chat. At first she did not mind answering Tim's questions, but then it appeared that for every question she answered, Tim asked two more. To Isabella, this was not a conversation; they were not exchanging and sharing. To Tim, it was a great conversation because he was learning a lot more about Isabella. She felt disconnected. He felt connected. A few weeks later Tim called and left a message, and even though Isabella cared about him, she did not return his call because she did not want to repeat the experience of their last conversation.

THE KNOW-IT-ALL

Have you ever been in a conversation with someone who knows everything? To children, a person who knows everything is mystical and magical. But once you are beyond age eight, talking with someone who knows everything no longer offers mystique and magic; it instead leads to misery and madness.

Appearing to know it all helps some people feel safe in the world. Many of us live by the belief that knowledge is power; therefore, in order to feel less vulnerable, some of us go to great lengths to let other people know that we know a lot. Others believe, subconsciously, that in order to be valued by others we have to be worthy. Having knowledge about virtually everything provides a sense of worthiness and therefore a sense of value for many of us. Yet the way in which know-it-alls seek to feel safe and valued often impedes meaningful and satisfying interpersonal connections that are ultimately the greatest vehicles to experiencing the sense of value and security they seek.

Alex wanted to share with his coworker Harold some information about one of the company's most influential managers. Harold was applying for a position that would report to this manager, and Alex believed this information might help Harold make his decision about whether to take the job. Even though Alex and Harold were not especially close, Alex felt that this was such important information that he had to let him know. But each time Alex attempted to give him a piece of the information, Harold would say, "Oh yeah, I heard that before." Or "I already knew that." Finally Alex stopped trying. He never got to share the most important part of the news, that the manager had plagiarized his assistants' work. Alex knew that it was unlikely that Harold had actually known any of this beforehand, and he suspected that since Harold did not have all of the information he might make a decision he would regret. Alex just did not feel like fighting through Harold's know-it-all attitude to help him avoid a major pitfall.

THE PESSIMIST

There are a few things in life that lead me to run for cover: weather storms, guns in the hands of people who are out of control, and chronic pessimists. The first two have the potential to injure or kill physically, the third can injure or kill emotionally and spiritually. While the effects of pessimistic conversation may not be visible, the effects are long lasting and toxic. Because of the pain from past hurts and disappointments, pessimists are afraid to believe anything might work out alright in their current experience.

Randy commented to Manuel that he was glad that the weather had not been too hot that summer. Manuel replied, "But wait and see. The rest of the summer will probably be a scorcher." Randy's enjoyment of the weather they had been experiencing went completely unheard. Then Randy expressed that he was glad about the new salary system being put in place at work. Manuel contested that the new salary system was probably the result of a lawsuit filed against the company that forced the powers-that-be to put something better in place to avoid future lawsuits. Two more times Randy began a new topic with Manuel and each time, Manuel found something negative or foreboding to say. Randy gave up trying to talk with Manuel. Then, as Manuel began talking about things, Randy was not really listening. Manuel's pessimism derailed any chance of effective communication.

THE OVEREXPLAINER

This is one of the lethal listening styles I am most practiced at using. I have irritated more than my share of people by being an overexplainer. After listening to one sentence, overexplainers respond in paragraphs. As the paragraphs continue the conversation is co-opted from the person who needs you to listen to him. When overexplainers are asked questions, they respond with treatises, giving the background to the answer and general, as well as specific, applications. After a while, the person in conversation with an overexplainer may become irritated, frustrated, and no longer interested in talking. Overexplaining often sends the message that you believe your conversation partner is not smart enough to understand what you have to say unless you go over it again and again, and in the simplest terms.

Hyun was telling Barry about a difficult meeting she had with their supervisor. Barry proceeded to tell Hyun about more effective strategies for managing their manager. Hyun thought that they were great ideas and said that she would try some of them. Then Barry explained the same things two more times in different ways. After the third time, Hyun commented to Barry, "Believe it or not, I really *do* understand English, Barry." Hearing her remark, Barry asked himself if all Asians were as sensitive as Hyun. Hyun assumed that Barry tended to overexplain to her because she was from Korea. Hyun didn't know that Barry overexplains to everybody. Barry, unaware that he overexplains to people, could not understand what Hyun was upset about, when he was only trying to help.

Having useful information overexplained becomes very irritating and insulting to most people. When it occurs across cultural, racial, ethnic, or gender lines, we often make the assumption that the other person overexplained because of prejudice or stereotyping. That may or may not be the case. Most overexplainers tend to act without regard to national origin, race, ethnicity, gender, sexual orientation, physical ability, age, or religion. Some overexplainers, however, are more likely to overexplain to people within certain groups than they are to others.

THE QUICK-FIXER

Often in our eagerness to love and support people as we are listening to them, we prematurely assess what they need and begin to give help that is neither needed nor desired. In the process, we accomplish the opposite of what we seek to do. Instead of bonding with others, we alienate them. Premature assessment and premature help create unsafe environments and thwart the likelihood of meaningful connections.

My father often showed his love by trying to safeguard me, his only daughter, from the struggles of life. When I was in my early twenties, I was sharing with my parents my decision to leave my job. I told them my reasons for leaving: I knew I had been set up for failure by my managers because of their racism, and I was in a no-win situation. My decision to leave, although scary, felt very right. I was expecting my parents to offer their sympathy and even express their anger about my situation. Instead, my father offered a laundry list of reasons that I should stay on the job and how the situation could be fixed. He did not hear, or at least never addressed, the pain I was experiencing in that job. Not feeling heard by him, I felt unsafe and became defensive. As a consequence, I could not hear the advice that he offered. The messages that I got from my father that day were: First, I should "get over" my feelings and stay in the job at all costs; and, second, I was not smart enough to make good choices for my life. I am certain that these were not the messages he intended to send, but because he moved too quickly to fix the situation by offering his advice, he accomplished the opposite of his intention to help me. Years later, I began to recognize that my father's inability to deal with my feelings regarding the racism I experienced on my job may have been directly related to his pain from the racism he too experienced at work. Even today, the wounding messages from that experience with my dad are triggered when people are too quick to offer advice without first acknowledging my feelings.

THE SELF-PROTECTOR

Effective listening involves maintaining healthy boundaries. Good boundaries can ensure that the listener does not become overly identified with the other person's concerns. When the balance of good boundaries is not achieved, however, one possible effect is that the listener responds in a self-protective manner, thus placing the focus of the conversation on himself or herself rather than on the concerns of the speaker. Such a conversation is almost certain to collapse and die.

TJ, for example, was telling Dorothy about an experience he had with Harry, a coworker, the previous week. Harry had treated TJ rudely, leaving TJ feeling uncomfortable and upset. As he told the story, Dorothy wondered if TJ was using it as a subtle way of conveying to her that she was rude and insensitive. The more she listened, the more defensive she became. She decided that TJ was probably blowing the entire situation out of proportion. So she told TJ, "I've never seen Harry behave rudely. Maybe you need to stop carrying your feelings on your shoulders all the time." TJ reminded Dorothy that she said the same thing about Harry a few weeks earlier. Dorothy simply frowned and waved her hand at TJ to dismiss his comment. TJ felt confused and betrayed, and the conversation came to an abrupt end.

TEN COMMON LISTENING BEHAVIORS

Ten common listening behaviors can often be seen at work alongside any of the lethal listening styles. Together, these lead to listening breakdowns and meltdowns.

1. listening to your own thoughts more than hearing the person talking
2. ignoring the emotions being expressed
3. assuming you know what the speaker will say before he or she says it
4. focusing exclusively on what the speaker expresses without factoring in nonverbal signals, such as tone of voice, pitch, body language
5. focusing solely on how the speaker expresses through nonverbal signals without attending closely to the content of what is being said
6. intertwining residual feelings from your previous interactions with the speaker
7. associating feelings from prior situations unrelated to the current speaker
8. projecting your feelings onto the speaker
9. assuming everybody expresses their thoughts and feelings the way you do

10. using one interpersonal language—intellectual or emotional—exclusively, despite clear cues from the speaker that that interpersonal language does not work best for him or her

What many of these behaviors have in common is that their focus on what is happening inside the thoughts and feelings of the listener. The history and hopes, experiences and expectations, fears and foibles of each of us as listeners greatly determine the extent to which communication moves toward either breakdown or breakthrough.

Being attentive to how you listen is key to engaging with others in life-giving ways. Often we use lethal listening styles because we put our listening activity on "automatic pilot." Sometimes we tend to use lethal listening styles because we only know how to use the listening styles that we have observed, or because we never knew that how we listen has a tremendous impact on the lives of every person with whom we interact. The reality is that how we listen does influence the transactional, relational, emotional, and spiritual levels of people's lives. With this in mind, continue journeying with me as we move toward emotional and spiritual strategies for more effective listening behaviors.

REFLECTION ACTIVITIES

1. Think of a frustrating conversation you have had, one that broke down because you felt unheard. What were the specific listening style(s) used by your listener? In your journal or in the back of this book, describe the behaviors.

Situation:
Analyst:
Co-Optor:
Drifter:
Interrupter:
Interrogator:
Know-It-All:
Pessimist:
Overexplainer:
Quick-Fixer:
Self-Protector:

2. What listening styles are most annoying to you? Why?

3. What are you most likely to do when you encounter someone whose listening styles irritate you?

4. Which listening style(s) best describe you. Describe the behaviors you observe in yourself that indicate that particular listening style.
   Analyst:
   Co-Optor:
   Drifter:
   Interrupter:
   Interrogator:
   Know-It-All:
   Pessimist:
   Overexplainer:
   Quick-Fixer:
   Self-Protector:

5. Compare your list of the listening styles most annoying to you and those you use most often. What are your observations?

6. To what extent does your listening style vary with different people or different environments?
   Listening style used more often with
      spouse/partner:
      children:
      parents:
      coworkers:
      classmates:
      friends:

   Listening style used more often
      at home:
      at work:
      at school:
      in religious/faith community contexts:
      in civic organizations:

FIVE
THE TRILOGY OF FEAR: FIGHT, FLIGHT, AND FREEZE

~

Whoever can see through all fear will always be safe.
—*Tao te Ching,* No. 46

Several years ago I was having a very difficult conversation with my friend Lillie when all of a sudden I wanted to get out. Not only out of the conversation, but out of the room. Suddenly, I felt my heart race and my temperature rise. As respectfully as possible, I asked if we could continue our conversation later. When Lillie kept insisting that we needed to work through our difficulties right then, I just got up and left.

Once out of the room and away from Lillie, I was able to examine why it had been so urgent for me to leave. I realized that I did not feel that Lillie was really listening to me, and when I feel that way I become fearful and feel unsafe. Then I remembered lots of other conversations in which, feeling fearful and unsafe, I had physically left the conversation space. I have a pattern of fleeing.

The distance created by fleeing is not necessarily physical distance. If I cannot get away physically, then I will create an emotional or intellectual distance. I may even take my thoughts away to other places and times so that I do not have to continue sharing the same space with the person who "caused" me to feel unsafe and afraid.

There are three general responses to fear: fight, flight, and freeze. No one *causes* us to have particular feelings or emotional responses. Each of us chooses to respond to certain circumstances or stimuli based on who we are, not based on what the other person does or does not do. In communication, our responses are related to the circumstances surrounding the conversation:

~

- our relationship with the person with whom we are talking
- our prior experiences that feel similar to the present interaction
- the issues being discussed
- how much information we have about what we perceive to be happening
- the physical environment in which the conversation occurs.

As any of these elements change, individual responses also change. But even with all these factors at play, most of us have a response-to-fear pattern that we use most often. Our preferred response pattern is based on individual personality and how safe we generally feel in the world.

For example, when Hannah told her thirty-seven-year-old twin sons, Joshua and Jeremiah, that she had decided to move to another state, each son responded differently. Joshua insisted that his mother was being hasty and showing disregard for her role as grandmother to his children. He spoke louder and louder to express his points, fighting verbally. Jeremiah, on the other hand, began by praising Hannah for finally making the decision to do something she had talked about for the five years since her husband died. Then he began thinking about the fact that his mother was getting older, and if she moved it would make it more challenging for him to care for her as her needs changed. Abruptly, in the middle of the conversation, Jeremiah excused himself and left the room to make an important phone call. In their hearts, both sons knew that this move would add joy to their mother's life. Their choices to fight or flee came in response to their shared fear of being abandoned by their mother.

Each of the fear responses—to fight, to flee, and to freeze—has distinctive characteristics and can be manifested both verbally and nonverbally. It is helpful for a listener to be able to identify the characteristic behaviors of these fear responses in order to recognize signals that the other partner in the conversation does not feel safe.

It is also helpful to recognize these behaviors in yourself, when you are not feeling safe in a conversation. In the intense emotion-packed moments that come with some conversations, it is easy to get sidetracked by responding to your own unconscious feelings of fear or anger. Knowing the behaviors that indicate the presence of fear can help you keep in touch with your own feelings of fear, and can enable you to make choices that will help the conversation feel safer for you and your conversation partner. Before we look more closely at the three responses to fear, we will explore fear itself.

FEAR AND SURVIVAL

Survival is a primal concern for every living creature, including, of course, human beings. Fear is a natural mechanism that helps preserve our physical and emotional well-being. Our inborn fear responses become activated if we perceive—consciously or unconsciously—that someone or something is a threat to our well-being or survival. In the context of communication, fear shapes and shades what we hear and how we respond.

In every moment, our minds take in information from the environment to assess our relative safety and well-being. Anything or anyone perceived as a threat to survival generates fear, and fear directs us to protect ourselves. Fighting, fleeing, or freezing are key ways we protect ourselves. You may respond to these self-protective messages by fighting, fleeing, or freezing in the midst of interactions, without any conscious awareness that you are doing so. Understanding this reality is critical to soul listening and to restoring communication that breaks down because of fear.

Because the human mind is so focused on protection and survival, it makes quick assessments about what seems safe, and often identifies a person or thing as a threat based on initial and incomplete information. Your mind rarely takes time to collect complete information about the perceived threat, and so does not assess the accuracy of the initial impression before sending the signal to self-protect. A memory of a harmful situation that looks similar to the present one may trigger a fear response. As a consequence, there are times when you or your conversation partner may respond to something said with inexplicable fear or anger because of an association with a prior, unrelated relationship or conversation.

It does not take an actual physical threat to activate fear responses. Fear response is prelingual and prerational, which means that it operates on a more basic, instinctual, primal plane than words and intellectual reasoning. Consequently, you might try to reason with yourself that there is nothing to be afraid of, but your primal response tells you to protect yourself. Once fear is triggered by a perceived threat, reason does not easily redirect or quiet that fear. In later chapters, we will explore ways of quieting fears so that you can soul listen.

As a listener you have a vital role to foster an environment for conversation that feels safe both for yourself and your conversation partners. If you begin to feel afraid, for whatever reasons, your ability to soul listen or connect with others is greatly impeded. If it doesn't feel safe, you will almost instinctively resort to a fight, flight, or freeze response in order to regain a sense of safety—even at the expense of significant relationships.

FIGHT BEHAVIORS

To illustrate the behaviors often present with the fight response, let me share a story about Doug and Kim. Recently, Kim came home from work with mixed feelings about a long-awaited promotion. She was thrilled about the promotion and its new responsibilities and possibilities. While many coworkers were celebrating her promotion, other coworkers were distracted by the false claims about Kim that another woman—who had unsuccessfully applied for the job—was spreading. This woman alleged that Kim had provided sexual favors to get the job. Kim's day was stressful—filled with both celebrating her promotion and dealing with the anger and false accusations made by the other applicant, who was now Kim's supervisee. Additionally, Kim had meetings throughout the day to plan for a major conference that was now her responsibility to oversee.

Because of all of the activity of the day, Kim forgot to return a phone message from her mother-in-law. At the end of the long and intense day, she went straight home to tell Doug about her promotion. Doug was not there, so after waiting for a half hour, Kim called Doug's work number, but he was not there either. Then she called a friend of Doug's from work, who told her that he thought Doug had gone home. After another half hour, she called her mother-in-law to find out if she had talked with Doug. To Kim's surprise, Doug answered the phone.

Kim exclaimed, "Hi, honey, there you are! I've been looking all over for you."

Doug replied, "Of course this is where I am. My mother fell. That's why she called you this morning—to ask you to come over to help her. I was out of the office and she couldn't reach me so she called her *dutiful* daughter-in-law. You know that she only has the two of us. Why didn't you call her back? It could have been a horrible emergency."

The conversation continued:

Kim: "I am so sorry. How is she?"

Doug: "Sorry? That's all you have to say? It has been seven hours since Mom called you. What were you doing today that you could not have returned the call before now?"

Kim: "Look, Doug. I said that I am sorry. Are you going to tell me how she is doing, or not?"

Doug: "She's fine, *now*. Fortunately, one of her neighbors came to visit and *she* helped my mother."

Kim: "Look, Douglas, I said I was sorry. I was extremely busy today and I don't need this from you."

Doug: "That's all you have to say? Mom could have been much more seriously hurt—"

Kim: "But she wasn't, Doug. So get off it—"

Doug: "Would you 'get off it' if this were your mother?"

Kim: "All right, Douglas, you've gone far enough. I am sorry that I can't drop what I am doing every time your mother needs help. I am sorry that I can't always fill in for you when you are not available."

Doug: "You're sorry all right."

Kim: "Don't blame it on me because you feel bad that you weren't there when she fell. Right now, I am sorry that I am talking with you—"

Doug: "You're sorry all right. You're not the only one who has had a rough day. There you go again. Always trying to push your guilt onto me. I never asked you to drop everything you're doing. But don't worry about it; I won't ask for your help with my mother again."

Kim: "Douglas, don't go there. Don't say anything else you'll regret."

Doug: "I'm sorry I expected that I could count on support from my wife—"

Kim: "I told you that I've had a rough day. I don't need this from you. And I'm not going to take it anymore—"

Doug: "But I see now, you'll help if you aren't having too bad a day, if it's convenient. I'll tell Mom to plan—"

Kim slammed down the phone before Doug could complete his sentence.

Both Kim and Doug respond to their fears with fighting. Let's look at the specific emotions and behaviors present in Kim and Doug's conversation. Doug was very worried about his mother. As Kim suggested, Doug was feeling guilty that he was not available when his mother was hurt. He was afraid that as his mother continues to age, she will need more assistance. He felt overwhelmed at the thought of caring for his mother alone. He expected that Kim would help him. His mother's fall also reminded him that his mother will die one day. He felt that when his mother dies, he will be all alone in the world. He had all of these feelings and did not know what to do with them. He was, perhaps, not even aware of most of these feelings. His rational self knew that there had to be a solid reason for Kim not to return a call to his mother, but his reason and common sense were blocked by his fears. As a result, Doug made comments about Kim that are not consistent with what he knows about her. He was emotionally disconnected from his knowledge of Kim's deep love for his mother. Because of his fear, he also made statements that generally do not fit his personality. For example, he made a hurtful jab at Kim by saying, "if this were your mother," knowing that Kim still struggled with issues regarding her own mother's death a few years earlier.

When Kim first heard Doug's voice she was excited and even relieved that at last she was talking with him. She had been waiting all day to tell him about her promotion, and was eager to talk with him about it. Kim just wanted to celebrate. When Doug told her about his mother, Kim was genuinely worried. She loves her mother-in-law. She too felt very guilty that she had not called her mother-in-law back. When Doug kept responding to Kim with his fear, manifested as anger, Kim felt that Doug completely disregarded her love for her mother-in-law. She felt that Doug was not listening to her and was not giving her any room to explain what happened. She also felt very unsafe in the conversation because she recognized that Doug was trying to transfer his sense of guilt onto her. The only way Kim knew how to protect herself in this situation was to fight back. She did so by using information that she knew or intuited about Doug's guilt. She slammed this information in his face in an effort to protect herself. While her assessment of Doug's guilty feelings was accurate, she expressed herself combatively and so could not be effectively helpful, loving, or supportive of Doug or their relationship. When Kim's fear and anger were triggered, her knee-jerk reaction was to protect herself at all costs. Her ability to express the love and support that Doug really needed was impeded by her fear. Kim did not have the ability to both fight and nurture Doug at the same time.

While the fight response is manifested in angry words and tones, what really underlies the anger is fear. Specific behaviors that often accompany the fight response, like those demonstrated by Doug and Kim, include:

- getting stuck or fixated on a single point
- interrupting constantly
- blaming others for almost everything
- being emotionally disconnected from one's own feelings
- ignoring the "facts" known about another person or the situation
- changing from a person who is reasonable and easy to talk with to someone who does not listen at all
- bringing up unresolved issues from prior conversations
- referring to hurtful experiences from other relationships
- using information about a loved one that is likely to be hurtful to him or her
- saying things that are not consistent with one's beliefs
- fidgeting and using frequent, jerky motions.

This list is not exhaustive, but does provide some common behaviors that demonstrate a fight response to feeling unsafe in a conversation. As you recognize these behaviors, remember that the fight response is motivated by an urgent need for protection, and not by malice or ill will toward you, the listener.

FLIGHT BEHAVIORS

Like the fight response, flight is a way to ensure survival in the face of a perceived threat. Some of us regard the fight response as the response of strong people and flight as the response of weak people. Others assume that fight is the preferred response of all males and that females prefer the flight response. Fighting is neither more emotionally strong nor innately male. Nor is fleeing more weak or female. Fear responses are not based on gender or emotional constitution. Developed early in life, our fear response patterns are influenced by our family and social environments. We develop behavior patterns that help us feel safe as quickly and for as long as possible. To illustrate what the flight response might look like, here is a story about Arleeta, Rashad, and Geraldine.

Arleeta and Rashad have been married for several years. Throughout their marriage, there has been a strained relationship between Arleeta and her mother-in-law, Geraldine. Rashad's father died when Rashad was only two years old, and Geraldine raised the children by herself. Rashad, the youngest of seven children, is very close to his mother. As a close-knit family, Geraldine's children, their spouses, and grandchildren come to her house every Sunday for dinner and a family evening together. Because Geraldine now lives alone and is retired, these times together with her family are the high point of her week. These Sunday evenings give Geraldine the opportunity to cook for her children, be involved in their lives, and give and receive much love. It appears that all of Geraldine's daughters- and sons-in-law, except Arleeta, have reasonably good relationships with her.

For Arleeta, this entire arrangement feels like a weekly command performance that she, Rashad, and their children must attend. Arleeta perceives Geraldine to be controlling and manipulative. Because of the required attendance on Sundays, Arleeta has missed many special events with her own family and friends. She has been trying to discuss her feelings and her needs with Rashad for years, but he has not supported her in her desire to do other things some weeks. Finally, Arleeta resolved that she would not continue this arrangement and decided to tell her husband and mother-in-law.

Arleeta began the conversation, "Mother Geraldine, I hope you know that I really appreciate all of the work that you do every week in preparing these meals for us. But I need to spend more time with my other family and friends also, sometimes on Sundays. So from now on, I won't be coming here every Sunday, but once or twice a month, instead. I've discussed this with Rashad already. Right, Rashad?"

Rashad responded, "We *began* talking about it. I didn't know that you felt this strongly—"

Geraldine interrupted her son. "What do you mean? Not come here every Sunday? You are part of this family. Sundays are family day. *Everybody* comes! It's the only time we have together. My *other* daughters-in-law want to be here and they are able to arrange time on the other six days of the week to be with other people. I am only asking for a few hours per week. Rashad, is this what you want, too?"

Rashad said, "Of course not, Mom. I'll be here. But—but, I think that this is a conversation between the two of you."

"Rashad," Arleeta said, "what do you mean that you didn't know I felt this strongly? We have been talking about this—no, I have been talking to you about this for at least three years. And, no, this is not just a conversation between your mother and me; this involves you, too. How could it not?"

Geraldine said, "So, you two have been talking about this for three years and no one ever bothered to say anything to me? Maybe if you had, we could have worked something out all of these years. Rashad, why didn't you say something to me, even if she didn't?"

"Look, Mom. I want to be here every week. Isn't that enough? And I'll make sure that the children and I are here. Beyond that I really think that this is something that you and Arleeta need to work out by yourselves. You are two grown women, you can figure it out for yourselves."

"You are my son," said Geraldine. "I thought I raised you to be honest and to share what's on your heart and mind with me. Why didn't you say anything to me?"

"Whatever your issues are, they don't involve me. Besides, I need to start the grill so that we can eat." Rashad rushed out of the room and into the backyard, leaving Arleeta and Geraldine by themselves.

In this conversation, both the fight and flight responses are present. We will focus on flight. From the outset of this conversation,

Rashad was ready to flee. His first effort was to deny his full knowledge of the depth of Arleeta's feelings. Then he insisted that the problem was not his, and therefore, he did not need to participate in the discussion. He tried to focus on the fact that Arleeta and Geraldine were both grown and able to resolve the situation without his help. Finally, he used his role as grill master as an excuse to get away. Rashad consciously or unconsciously perceived this as a no-win situation between the two women he loved most, his mother and his wife. He felt that anything he said in support of one would anger or hurt the other. The bleak-looking options evoked a lot of anxiety for Rashad. For the sake of his own survival, he decided that the best thing to do was to leave the situation quickly.

Flight is not Rashad's only response pattern. As the youngest of seven children, Rashad learned early to fight—physically and verbally—to defend himself against his older siblings. But with his mother, running away was the only way to safety. Fighting was not an option with his mother, for he feared it might hurt her. Rashad brought this behavior pattern to his relationship with his wife as well. Feeling doubly unsafe with the two women most important in his life, his need to flee felt even more urgent. Even though Rashad was not aware of it, these unconscious feelings of fear and anxiety determined his choices. He could not really listen deeply to Geraldine or Arleeta because he was focused on protecting himself from the anger he anticipated from them.

To help you recognize when you or someone else may be feeling afraid, here is a list of common behaviors that indicate a flight response:

- ending the conversation abruptly
- redirecting the focus of the conversation
- remembering something else that must be immediately attended to
- suddenly becoming very tired or sleepy
- refusing to talk anymore
- intellectualizing and separating from emotions
- insisting that either there is no problem or the problem is not yours
- becoming very quiet, perhaps even silent

- telling people what they want to hear even if it is not true
- focusing on analyzing the other person
- fidgeting and jerky body movements.

FREEZE BEHAVIORS

These first two survival responses to fear—fight and flight—are joined by a third, also common response: freeze. Some animals respond to threats by freezing in place with the intention of becoming so unrecognizable—not seen, heard, or smelled—that the potential source of danger will go away. Some human beings do the same. For most of us, the freeze response is not so calculated. We freeze because we are so gripped by fear and anxiety that we cannot think clearly, cannot speak, and cannot move. To illustrate this, here are the highlights of a conversation that Kirk had with his old friend Jimmy.

Kirk and Patricia recently announced that they were going to get married in four months. Now that the wedding date is less than two months away, Kirk's buddies have begun pressuring him about who he is going to ask to be his best man. Kirk's marriage with Patricia will be his second marriage. After he decided who would be best man for his first wedding, some of the friends who were not asked became somewhat distant from him. Jimmy, in particular, felt that Kirk had shunned him. Sensing this, Kirk had said jokingly, "Jimmy, if this one doesn't work and I ever get married again, you know you'll be the best man. You'll be the man." Twelve years later, with Kirk preparing to get married again, Jimmy called Kirk to remind him about that promise.

Jimmy: "Kirk, I'm ready. Now, I didn't want you and Yolanda to break up just so that I could be your best man the second time around, but since it happened, I am here and I am at your service."

Kirk remains silent, so Jimmy continues: "You're not going to let me down a second time are you?"

Kirk: "Uh, wow, man. I don't know what to say. Uh, you still want to do that, as old as we are?"

Jimmy: "Yeah, man. I'm ready. If you had had me as the best man the first time around, maybe things would have worked out with you and Yolanda. But since that didn't work, I'm your man."

Kirk: "Oh. Uh, Patricia and I are planning a very small ceremony. We still haven't decided whether or not we are going to have any wedding attendants."

Jimmy: "Yeah, but you have to have two witnesses sign the papers. And I would be honored to be one of them and stand up there with you. Man, we go way back. We have a long history together. And I am proud of you for being brave enough to try this marriage thing again. Standing up there might inspire me to try it for the *first* time. That is, unless you are reneging on your promise. You aren't doing that, are you?"

Kirk: "Uh, me renege on a promise I made to you? You are like a big brother to me."

Jimmy: "Well, then what's the problem? I don't hear you giving me any information about my part in the wedding. And I don't hear you saying things like, 'Jimmy, I am glad you are still here with me to stand with me and participate in this special event.' Or, 'Come on, let's go select the tuxedos.' How come I don't hear you saying any of that? Did you ask one of your new boys? Because if you did, I just need you to say that and I'll get the picture. And you won't have to worry about me in this wedding or your life ever again."

Kirk: "I don't know what to say, Jimmy. No, I did not ask any of my new friends. Patricia and I just haven't decided on the details yet. That's all."

Jimmy: "Look, man, I've got to go. Call me back later as soon as you and Patricia have made your plans."

Kirk: "Yeah, sure."

In this scenario, Kirk does not want to hurt his childhood buddy, yet he does not want him to be his best man. Kirk is torn about what to do. Patricia has been reminding him for weeks that he needs to make a decision about his best man, but he keeps putting it off. Because Jimmy, Kirk, and Kirk's first wife Yolanda all grew up together, Kirk does not want people in his wedding who are associated with Yolanda. Because he is, in reality, nervous about getting married again, it is very important to him to have a clean, fresh start with Patricia. He feels that if there are too many of his longtime friends from the "'hood," it will make it even harder to achieve a clean start. Kirk, in the confusion brought on by Jimmy's directness, freezes. Just the night before, Kirk had decided to call Jimmy and invite him to lunch so that they could talk. But when Jimmy called, he caught Kirk off guard, and Kirk forgot his plan. Because Jimmy initiated the discussion and confronted Kirk very directly, Kirk became emotionally and intellectually frozen and was unable to take advantage of this opportunity to handle the situation.

Kirk developed a pattern of freezing when he was a little boy. This pattern shows up primarily in confrontations with people he loves. Much of it stems from fears that are rooted in his father's alcoholism. Drinking caused tremendous personality changes in Kirk's father. When sober, his father was quiet and gentle; when drinking, he was very loud and combative. The change in his father was so stark that Kirk often became emotionally frozen, and at times physically immobile, when confronted by his father. This fear response continues in his personal life today. At work, Kirk is very commanding and deals with problems directly. But with problems in the context of his intimate relationships, especially those that are long-term, Kirk freezes.

Jimmy, fearing that Kirk did not want him in the wedding, responded by fleeing when he hinted that he would end the conversation and his involvement in Kirk's life if that was what Kirk wanted.

Common indicators of the freeze response include:
• inability to express thoughts or feelings
• inability to make a decision
• babbling—saying words that make little sense
• providing little or no information
• being less articulate than usual
• misremembering or not remembering prior events or conversations
• contradicting things said earlier in the same conversation
• looking glazed or staring into space
• being emotionally disconnected from one's own feelings
• becoming very quiet, perhaps even silent
• crying, but being unable to express why.

As illustrated in the examples above, when we do not feel safe in conversations, we will say or do almost anything to regain a sense of safety as quickly as we can. We seek safety by fighting the perceived threat, fleeing it, or freezing in place. When these responses to fear are at work, however, the conversation cannot be productive.

Our conversation partners are more likely to demonstrate fight, flight, or freeze responses when we as listeners use one or more of the lethal listening styles presented in chapter 4. While there is no guarantee that your conversation partners will always feel safe with you, by avoiding lethal listening styles you will minimize the likelihood of fight, flight, and freeze responses from your partner and yourself.

Avoiding lethal listening styles is an important first step toward creating environments for conversation that nurture and listen people's souls into greater life. A second important step is understanding and recognizing the presence of the fear responses of fight, flight, and freeze, from both your conversation partner and yourself. The third step, listening to your own soul, will be explored more fully in part III.

REFLECTION ACTIVITIES

1. Based on the behavior indicators for fight, flight, and freeze responses, which response is your most common when you feel unsafe in conversations? What behaviors indicate this response?

2. Name the three to five people with whom you have most of your conversations.
    a.   What fear response does of each of these individuals seem to use most? What behaviors lead you to your conclusion?
    b.   What do you feel and do in response to their common fear responses?

3. Think about a recent conversation that ended in a communication breakdown. Refer to the behaviors commonly exhibited as part of fight, flight, or freeze responses to fear.
    a.   Which, if any, fear response(s) did you recall seeing from your conservation partner?
    b.   What were the specific behaviors you observed?
    c.   What was occurring in the conversation when you began observing these behaviors?
    d.   Knowing what you know thus far, what might you do to help foster a sense of safety if a similar situation occurs?

Six
The Breakdown of Trust

~

My ego is like a fortress.
I have built its walls stone by stone
To hold out the invasion of the love of God.
    —Howard Thurman, *"I Let Go of My Accumulations"*

T rust is one of the hardest emotions to experience and hold on to. By the time most of us are adults, we have been disappointed and hurt so many times that we are afraid to trust others fully. Distrust in others leads us to build higher and higher walls of self-protection. When we focus on protecting ourselves, not only do we block out potential hurt, we also prevent potential interaction that satisfies our longing for true intimacy. Lack of trust—whether in other people, God, or even ourselves—blocks our ability to listen. Because of distrust, we often interpret what we hear based on our fear of being hurt rather than on what is actually being said.

The Limiting Power of Overgeneralizations

It is critical, for the sake of safety and well-being, to know whom to trust. When devoid of trust, however, relationships—with ourself, others, and God—cannot develop and grow. To listen *into* the soul and *with* the soul, trust is essential.

Distrust is a defense we use to protect ourselves from potential pain. Often, however, the situation or person that resembles the past source of pain is not necessarily a source of pain now. As children learning our way in the world, we generalize every experience, especially experiences in which our trust is broken. Because of these generalizations, each time a person, especially someone significant in our lives, breaks our trust, we begin to generalize a belief that

~

most people are not trustworthy. Our childhood generalizations unconsciously direct many of our choices in adulthood, and shape and shade how we listen.

Here is an example of how generalized experiences from the past shape our ability to trust and to listen. When Miriam was a little girl, her grandmother died while away on vacation. As a child, Miriam grew to believe that when people say they are going on a trip, they really mean that they are going to die. Now thirty-four years old, Miriam knows that taking a trip is not a euphemism for death, but she still gets nervous when any of her loved ones travel for more than three days in a row. Miriam's husband, John, travels a lot with his job, often for five to ten days at a time. Miriam asks him to call home every day to reassure her that he is alive and safe.

To John, however, the demand for a daily phone call feels like Miriam is checking up on him. John assumes that Miriam suspects him of being sexually involved with other people while he is out of town. He feels that she doesn't trust him enough to know that he is faithful to their relationship. In fact, Miriam does trust John to be faithful to their marriage. Miriam just doesn't trust John not to die.

Although Miriam has tried to explain the root of her concern to John, he has not believed her. John's background contributes to his distrust of Miriam's motives. His past experience has conditioned him to suspect any inquiries about his whereabouts and activities as an indication that he is not trusted. As a teenager, whenever John came home late his mother accused him of having sex with girls. Although he was not sexually active, his mother punished him based on her assumptions. Now each time Miriam asks him to call, it reminds John of his mother's distrust of him. John has generalized that all women are like his mother. He does not trust Miriam to tell him the truth about what he has convinced himself she is really thinking.

Because of their respective trust issues, John and Miriam are not really able to listen to and hear one another. Because of the overgeneralizing they both do, they are constantly trying to protect themselves from potential hurts. Everything they hear each other say is filtered through their fears. Miriam and John really love one another, but they do not know what to do to strengthen their trust.

Three steps can interrupt distrust based on overgeneralizations from past disappointments and injuries. First, listen to your soul to learn about the origin of your overgeneralized feelings of fear, hurt, anger, and so on. You may not have conscious awareness of what injured you, but at the soul level it is not specific information that you need.

Second, honor the pain and grieve the loss you incurred in the original situation. Perhaps, like many people, you have convinced yourself that it didn't hurt that badly. Until you acknowledge the power of the original pain, the pain has power over you.

Third, recognize that the original situation and the people involved in it did not have the power to injure you irreparably or eternally. That is, you can heal and recover from your pain. You have the power to move through and release the pain. You can only get to step three after accomplishing steps one and two. Without moving through these three steps, you remain emotionally blocked and spiritually bound. Emotionally, you are impeded from trusting others in the ways that foster growth and wholeness. Spiritually, being bound by a belief system based in pain and distrust does not allow you to fully know and express who you are.

Back to John and Miriam. While Miriam already has some insight into her fear of John dying, if she listened more deeply into her own soul, she also might be able to hear her soul telling her that by choosing to marry a man who travels a lot she has given herself a great opportunity to work through and release her fear of abandonment. And she might hear her soul telling her that John is not her grandmother. She can let herself fully grieve her grandmother's death and thank her grandmother for loving her so unconditionally that it helped prepare her heart to receive John's love and to love him unconditionally. Finally, Miriam might hear her soul remind her that she is and will be safe even if John dies. Once Miriam reaches this point, she can live more fully, celebrating each moment they have together instead of fearing John's death.

As she hears and honors these messages, Miriam becomes better able to recognize her readiness to let go of her childhood generalization about death. Her awareness of her own readiness can enable Miriam to experiment by not requiring John to call for a few days. In preparation for such an experiment, Miriam asks John to partner with her in her healing process. She invites John to help her plan the experiment in ways that work for him. And she explains to John that because she feels so unconditionally loved by him that her anxiety in relation to him dying is very high and she thanks him for his love. Finally, Miriam listens to guidance from the Divine within her for ways to manage her feelings of anxiety during the time she does not talk with John.

Similarly, John has the opportunity to listen into his own soul and get more in touch with his generalized distrust of women. On his emotional surface, John is not aware that he does not trust Miriam to tell the truth. Miriam has always been open, honest, and truthful. These characteristics are part of why John loves her so much. John has never told Miriam about the punishment he received from his mother, and her refusal to trust him, because it is a painful memory. In addition, the only way John knows how to have a loving relationship with his mother is to suppress the hurt and anger associated with her. Even though he is not consciously aware of his feelings, each time Miriam asks John to call, his body gives him loud signals about his feelings, such as a pain that comes in his stomach. Listening to his body—messages from his soul—John can begin to recognize that these are familiar feelings that predate his years with Miriam. This information can help John get in touch with the experiences of these feelings during his youth, and to understand that these feelings are not just about Miriam. Even if he is not able to associate the feelings with his mother's distrust and punishment, John still becomes able to tell Miriam that this issue is bigger than their relationship and is triggered each time he is expected to call home. As Miriam and John attune themselves to and share the messages within their own souls, they are better able to build trust, take risks, and foster the healing needed within each of them and in their relationship.

It Matters Where You Place Your Trust

The challenges associated with trusting one another and the Divine are reflected across histories and cultures. For example, the story of the Tower of Babel, from Judeo-Christian scripture, tells of a community working to build a great city that includes a tower. In the course of their efforts, their one language becomes broken into many languages, and as a result they are no longer able to communicate, to really listen to and understand one another. Once this happens, they are no longer able to work together on their shared projects. They end up going their separate ways.

Theologians have typically interpreted this story to mean that by building the tower, these people were striving to be gods, and therefore their Creator God confounded their language to thwart their efforts. I want to offer a different interpretation of this story. That is, the Tower of Babel story underscores how critical trust is to communication and to productive relationships, and demonstrates that we need trustworthy communication with the Divine if we are to maintain healthy and productive relationships.

The story depicts people who had a shared dream. Because of their initial trust in each other, they were able to conceive a shared vision of a great city and a tall tower. Once they started their building project, they were so excited and passionate about their project that for a time their trust and respect grew. Part of what enabled them to trust each other was their ability to speak and understand the same language. At the beginning, they listened to and communicated with one another very well. Then, like most relationships, the relationship of the community at the Tower of Babel cycled through relationship stages. Here, described in terms of a one-to-one relationship, is my capsule version of the stages of trust in relationships.

Stage 1: You and your partner meet and immediately discover a deep connection. You have an uncanny, inexplicable sense of trust. You discover that you like the same foods, music, movies, books. You are committed to the same social and political issues. You can't think of a finer, smarter person you would rather talk with, work with, or just get to know. Your communication is somewhat tenuous and awkward at times, yet shows a lot of promise. A trust is established based on the emotional and spiritual levels each of you has in common. Generally, however, these levels are at the surface of each person's respective issues. Therefore, although it feels like the trust runs deep, it really only scratches the surface.

Stage 2: You and your partner are getting to know one another and building a sense of comfort. Because of this trust and respect, you and your partner decide to work on an important tower-building project together, such as planning a major social event, developing a business proposal, or becoming romantically committed. As your mutual project develops, you spend even more time together. You know that this is the person you have been waiting, longing, hoping, and praying for. You have complete trust in her. You feel that you can say anything to him. As the intimacy increases, you begin to open deeper levels of yourself to her. This sets the stage for the full exposure of core emotional and spiritual issues that you are not entirely aware of. Initially, you welcome this.

Stage 3: As the project proceeds, you begin noticing that your partner is changing. He is not as supportive and collaborative as he used to be. Or she is becoming more defensive. At times, you notice a certain competitive attitude that was not there before. Or you observe that he does not share his thoughts or feelings with you as easily as he did before. You realize that there are some control issues going on that you had not seen earlier. The focus and attention you used to give one another is now absorbed in your shared project. The trust that was so high before is at an all-time low. The quality of your communication erodes. You begin realizing that you speak in two different languages. When you are using the interpersonal language of feelings, your partner is using the language of intellect, and vice versa. Rarely are you speaking the same language at the same time. You begin operating more independently of one another because it feels more productive and less stressful. It seems as if someone or something came along and created tension between you, and neither of you knows what to do to change the situation.

Stage 4: After lots of attempts to keep working on your project, one or both of you decides to abandon it. You just cannot understand or trust one another anymore. Your dream to reach the heavens remains unrealized. You were halfway there, but you cannot go any further, any higher.

Trust is essential for relationships to deepen and grow. It is also critical for projects to move forward to successful completion. Yet giving trust produces anxiety for most people. After we have given it, we begin to feel vulnerable and unsafe. As a consequence of our sense of vulnerability, we have become defensive. We are likely to become more critically aware of every action taken and every word spoken by the ones in whom we put our trust, our *trustees*. Our expectations of how trustees speak, listen, intuit, and understand skyrocket. We often interpret any mistakes in judgment or inexact expression on the part of trustees as an indication of their untrustworthiness, especially if we are gripped by overgeneralizations from past hurts.

The Tower of Babel story suggests that when we put our trust and complete reliance in other human beings without the relationship being grounded in Divine guidance and collaboration in our projects, our relationships are likely headed for an overwhelming sense of vulnerability that leads to miscommunication and chaos. Overreliance on others, instead of the Divine, often leads to fear, which leads to distrust. Opening ourselves to others in such intimate ways without the ongoing practice of listening to our own souls leaves us with a sense of vulnerability, often too great to tolerate. Without ongoing, attuned listening to Divine guidance for ways to listen deeply to others, we end up retreating from intimacy into self-protection. What starts as an ideal relationship with the sense of really feeling heard and understood by one another becomes labored and confused communication with no one able to understand the other. Confusion. Distrust. And perhaps going separate ways.

Here's a workplace example of the impact of misplaced trust. Karla and Bill were colleagues at a medical equipment supply company that was experiencing a severe slump in its sales. Prior to the worst of the sales slump, they were developing a trusting work relationship. Once the sales continued to nosedive, their relationship quickly deteriorated to distrust and anger. As the marketing director, Karla was being blamed for decline in sales. Bill, the company's sales director, was also pointed to as responsible because he did not push his sales staff hard enough to get new business. Bill and Karla began to work closely together to turn the tide of the sales. At first, things were working favorably. Each of them wondered why they had not worked more closely all along. As the sales figures improved, they developed a high degree of trust for one another.

Their relationship took a sharp turn one month when sales figures declined again. One day, Karla and Bill met to develop a new strategy. Not long into their meeting, however, Karla became angry and ready to walk out of the meeting because Bill interrupted her almost every time she spoke. And not much of what he said made any sense to Karla. The more Bill talked, the more Karla asked herself why she had even bothered. She thought that at least she was making concrete recommendations. What was Bill offering? Why did she think that anything could really improve how she and Bill worked together?

Karla did her best to choose her words carefully so she would not appear judgmental. Nonetheless, she felt Bill did not accept his share of responsibility for the situation the company was in. Then, Bill began to blame Karla's department for the past month's sales results. At that point, Karla asked Bill if both of them could think more about possible strategies and get back to each other later. As she walked out of the meeting, Karla said to herself, "I'll show him." She was not willing to invest any more time trying to strengthen her working relationship with Bill. She knew her decision meant that *she* could not deliver her best performance, but she was willing to live with that consequence because trying to communicate and work with Bill was not worth the effort. She no longer trusted Bill to be a fair and responsible colleague upon whom she could rely.

So what happened? Three common things occurred. First, because they were both feeling so vulnerable, Karla interpreted that all of Bill's comments were underhanded statements about her, and Bill assumed that Karla's recommendations were designed to blame him. Second, because each assumed that the other was making underhanded comments about their work, their trust quickly eroded and both put up self-protective walls. They became ensnared in a web of distrust that neither knew how to escape. Third, because they both rooted their trust in each other without having sought inner guidance, when things did not work as smoothly as they expected, they began to speak different languages. Caught in their own emotional snags, communication quickly broke down. Because of their respective fears, neither was able to listen to and understand the other.

Both Karla and Bill felt unsafe because of the assumptions that each had made about the other. The more unsafe they felt, the more they fought. Some of the fighting was done in overt ways. Most of it was done covertly, in a passive-aggressive way, as is often the case in workplaces. Although neither Karla nor Bill looked like they were fighting, they fought one another until the company folded.

TRUSTING YOUR INNER WISDOM

If all of your trust is placed in the actions and words of another human being, it is extremely difficult, once that person disappoints you, to feel safe enough to listen to and understand what he is saying. And that's when you need trust the most. So it's important to build a trusting relationship with the wisdom of your own soul, which enables you to access Divine guidance. This trust enables you to be attuned to what is spoken beneath the surface.

Soul listening and trusting Divine guidance are strong foundations for building trusting relationships with others. To build or rebuild trust involves actively seeking the Divine to understand that our ultimate well-being relies not in others but in the divine creative Spirit.

Soul listening within yourself enhances your ability to create the sense of safety you need in order to be more vulnerable, fully present, and trusting in your relationships. As you feel safer, you are more able to listen from your soul. As you listen, you help create an environment in which both you and others can grow and be nurtured. When you entrust your well-being to Divine guidance, you have more time, energy, and love to fine-tune your listening.

REFLECTION ACTIVITIES

1. What do you think, feel, and do when you suspect that someone does not trust you?

2. What are some of the issues that you find difficult to trust other people with? What do you do to protect yourself and protect your interests?

3. In what ways have past hurts influenced your level of trust in the Divine? How does this, in turn, influence your ability to trust others?

4. To what extent does your trust or lack of trust in others influence your ability to trust the Divine?

5. Does the level of trust you currently have in others, in God, and in yourself promote life? To what extent does it satisfy your soul's needs?

6. There are three critical steps needed to overcome the emotionally and spiritually confining effects of overgeneralizations.
- listen to your soul to learn about the origin of your over-generalized feelings of fear, hurt, anger, shame, self-doubt
- honor the pain and grieve the loss you originally experienced
- recognize that the person who injured you cannot harm your soul, but that you have the power to move through and release the pain.

For the next weeks, journal about each of these three points and listen to what your soul is saying to you about how to move through the pain and be able to trust yourself, others, and God more fully.

SEVEN
INTERRUPTIONS TO YOUR FLOW

～

We must lend listening ears to the songs
and signs of life found in nature,
the events of history, and the social encounters
of our daily routine.
We never know when or how new meaning
might break through.
    —Andrew Young, *A Way Out of No Way*

P erhaps you are sometimes bewildered when a seemingly simple conversation ends abruptly because of hurt or angry feelings. Or confused when your conversation halts with one or both of you storming out of the room or hanging up the telephone. Or dismayed by conversations that result in silent pain and hurt—silent because no one has the words or sense of trust to discuss what you are feeling anymore. The conversation that was flowing so smoothly has hit an impenetrable barrier it cannot move beyond.

Here's an example of a simple conversation that hit a communication wall. Ariel has been the director of finance for a nonprofit youth services organization for the past two years. After being in meetings all day, Ariel was finally able to work on an important report that was due in one week. The report he was working on is part of a package of financial projections to be used by the board of directors in deciding whether the agency should purchase its own building. Right then, the financial projections did not look as favorable as they had when the agency first began exploring this vision. While Ariel was working on the report, Dominique, the manager of volunteer development, came to Ariel's office, saying she needed to talk with him about one of the volunteers. Dominique's questions for Ariel usually have to do with volunteers' travel reimbursements, so

～

Ariel assumed that was the subject of this conversation. Dominique said, "I have some great news from one of the volunteers about our building project." But Ariel was deep in thought about the report, and because he assumed he knew what Dominique wanted to talk about, he did not even hear the reference to the building project. Ariel responded in a condescending tone, "Dominique, I don't mean any harm, but I don't have time to talk with you right now about your volunteers. I'm working on something really important. I'll let you know when I can talk to you later."

Dominique responded, "But Ariel—"

Ariel sternly stated, "Dominique, I said I don't have time."

Insulted, Dominique stormed out of Ariel's office. Consequently, Ariel did not get the information until after the board meeting that a volunteer had offered to gift the agency with fifty percent of the purchase cost. While the agency was eventually able to take advantage of the volunteer's financial gift, they did not get the building they preferred because Ariel missed out on the information about the gift when Dominique first came to him.

How It All Starts

How do seemingly simple conversations become points of lost opportunity, impasse, raging anger, or silent pain? Is there any way to prevent these communication breakdowns? Is there any way to rescue these conversations? To explore these questions, let's look at a few scenarios that demonstrate how typical conversations begin.

Scenario 1: Interruptions. You are in your office or at home by yourself, finally getting to do the work or enjoying the quiet time you have anticipated for days, when all of a sudden it happens: somebody comes into the room or calls on the telephone and starts talking to you, breaking your precious moment of silence, disrupting the moment you have been craving. You are expected to shift gears quickly in order to be available to this interrupter. Part of you knows that this person—your student, coworker, spouse, friend, child, parent, client—does not intend to disrupt you, so you try to greet her warmly and ask what you can do to help.

Scenario 2: Changes in Direction. You and your spouse are spending some rare and precious time together. You have been looking forward to this time for weeks. The conversation is flowing so smoothly and easily that you are not being very particular about what you do or say, you are just enjoying the time together. Everything is going great. Then your spouse mentions something she has been waiting to talk with you about. You want to continue the easygoing conversation, but she wants to communicate something more difficult. It seems that she is having some struggle in expressing whatever the issue is. You are not quite certain what she is trying to say, so you say something that you think will help. Then, before you know it you are in an argument, and you cannot quite retrace how you got there.

Scenario 3: Hidden Agendas Revealed. You are asked by your boss to attend a meeting with a few other staff members to brainstorm ideas for a new project. Because the meeting is called a brainstorming session, you come in with some new ideas that you think will both help accomplish the goals of the organization and help strengthen your credibility among your colleagues. You come to the meeting thrilled that you are one of a handpicked team selected for this planning process. As the meeting progresses, you begin to identify a particular pattern as to which ideas are well received and which are not. You realize that this is not a brainstorming meeting at all, but rather a way for your boss to manipulate the process to get what she wants. At this point, feeling used and insulted, you no longer want to participate in a process that feels like a charade, but you understand that you must continue to contribute to the discussion.

Of course these three scenarios do not reflect all of the ways in which seemingly normal conversations end in communication shutdown. But they point out that conversations often begin as interruptions, in one way or another, to the flow of your activity, thoughts, or expectations. How you handle these interruptions largely determines the success of your ability to listen.

>

SHIFTING GEARS

Although most conversations begin as interruptions, some interruptions are welcome and others are not. The challenge is how to fully listen in conversations that are either unwelcome from the outset or become unwelcome as changes and turns take place.

Communication breaks down when the expectations or needs of the conversation partners and their perceived experiences in the conversation become disconnected—in other words, when we expect one thing from a conversation, but we get something that we feel is less desirable. It is almost impossible to enter conversations with no expectations or needs. Because of the expectations and needs we bring to our conversations, all communication has the potential to break down unless one or both conversation partners soul listen.

Whether you are enjoying precious time alone, relaxing with a loved one, or offering your ideas at work or home, when something happens in opposition to your expectations for that period of time, you may find yourself struggling to shift gears. Just as a car in the wrong gear will not perform effectively, if you are in the wrong "listening gear" you will not be an effective listener. Part of you may seek to listen and be supportive, yet another part of you wants to hurry back to the time you had planned. Your ability to shift gears depends on your answers to several questions:

1. What were your expectations regarding how you would spend your time?

2. How focused were you on what you were doing and thinking about prior to this new conversation?

3. How critical do you consider what you were doing or thinking about?

4. How likely does it seem that you will immediately be able to get back to what you were doing or thinking?

5. How relevant does the issue presented in this new conversation feel to you?

6. What are your feelings about your relationship with the interrupter?

7. What has your day looked like thus far?

8. What other things may be happening in your life and in your relationship with this conversation partner?

9. How able are you in general to accept changes or go with the flow?

10. What kinds of listening styles do you use and to what extent are these styles compatible with what your partner needs at the moment?

Your answers to these questions reflect your readiness to shift the flow of your activity, thoughts, or expectations in order to listen. If you resist the shift, you may miss the first ten to sixty seconds of conversation, during which some of the most important contextual information is given. You and your conversation partner are in danger of becoming engaged in two different conversations because you did not absorb some key information provided in the first minute of conversation. Being inadequately present in the conversation, you diminish your ability to engage in the conversation respectfully and efficiently, thus enabling you to return to your previous activity more quickly.

In this section, we have explored the adverse impact that lethal listening styles, fear responses, mistrust, and responses to interruptions can have on our abilities to listen. In the remaining chapters, we will explore how soul listening is a tool to avoid these adverse consequences and transform lethal listening behaviors to listening that fosters productive, respectful, and loving communication.

REFLECTION ACTIVITIES

1. Think about a recent conversation, initiated by someone else, that began smoothly yet ended roughly. What were you doing prior to this conversation? At the beginning of the conversation, what were your thoughts and feelings about what you wanted to do? Diagnose what happened within you as the conversation progressed.

2. Use the same process to diagnose what happened in two or three other rough conversations. Are there any patterns in your conversations? If so, what are they?

3. Make a list of five things you expect to receive from and five things you expect to be able to give to conversations. Review the conversations you diagnosed above and compare your list of expectations

with those problematic conversations. Compare your list of expectations with healthy, productive conversations you noted in the Reflection Activities for chapter 1.

Expect to Receive   Expect to Give
1.   1.
2.   2.
3.   3.
4.   4.
5.   5.

4. For the next week, if someone initiates a conversation with you, interrupting you in a moment of work or quiet, ask them to restate their first few sentences to ensure that you accurately hear their issue (alternatively, you may restate those sentences yourself). Record the new information you collect about how much you are able to hear while shifting gears into a conversation.

5. To strengthen your ability to go with the flow as conversations change direction, for the next week listen to water. Listen to water flowing in the shower, in the stream near your home, in the rain. Listen to the changes in the sounds of the water. For example, step into the shower and listen to the changing sound of the water as it hits your body and then flows to the floor. Write down any thoughts or feelings that emerge as you listen.

Part III: From Listening Breakdowns to Breakthroughs

~

Whoever is stiff and inflexible is a disciple of death.
Whoever is soft and yielding is a disciple of life.
—*Tao te Ching,* **No. 76**

~

Eight
It's All about Me

~

We do not see [and hear] things as they are; we see [and hear] things as we are.
   —The Talmud

Several years ago as I began examining how I interact with people, I discovered that I was still operating with the worldview of a two-year-old. That is, I kept imagining that virtually everything someone else said *really* had something to do with me.

Two-year-olds live in a world that revolves around them. As babies, they got attention, food, milk, or comfort when they cried. It is no wonder that little ones believe the world is here to satisfy their needs. They don't get much information to dispute that belief. And then the "everything is mine" phase of two-year-olds begins. Everything they see, hear, say, feel, and do is about them. Me. Mine. Everything.

One example of this occurred a couple of years ago when my friend Candas commented that she couldn't stand it when people talked pretentiously. Immediately—even though she was one of my closest friends—I *knew* that she was talking about me. I knew she was indirectly telling me that she couldn't stand how I speak. What she didn't know was that throughout my childhood I was often teased about the way I spoke. Because I was a dark-skinned African American child who spoke Standard English, some schoolmates accused me of "trying to talk white." Candas had unintentionally aggravated an unhealed wound and awakened painful memories. With all of this emotional stuff going on inside, I did the only thing I knew how to do: I became defensive and didn't hear much else that Candas had to say. I didn't tell her what I was thinking or feeling until several days later. To my surprise, she had not been talking about me at all. She cited examples of the people she had in mind.

~

Then she told me how much she loved how I speak. Once I shared how I had been teased during my childhood, she understood why I thought that she was talking about me. She was glad that I finally took the risk to tell her what I was feeling and thinking.

I had carried around anger and shame for several days because, like a two-year-old, I thought Candas's world revolved around me. For several days, I acted strange and distant toward my friend. During that time, I missed the opportunity to hear my friend tell me how much she loved to hear me speak. Once I heard how she felt about my speech, she helped in my healing process as I continued to let go of that childhood pain. I vowed then to keep moving beyond my terrible twos and to learn that, while I am very significant to many people, I am not the only person on their minds. I am not the center of their every thought or word.

In some ways, most of us continue to be like two-year-olds, thinking that everything revolves around us. To be fully present to others, it is critical to consider the possibility that what they are talking about is not centered on you.

MAKING THINGS UP TO FEEL SAFE

When we see people behave in certain ways, we make assumptions about their inner motivations and thoughts. Making up a set of somewhat plausible explanations for what we see provides us with a sense of safety that enables us to proceed through the uncertainties of life. Because uncertainty about the people and circumstances in our environments produces anxiety in most of us, we can create elaborate explanations and assumptions about what we hear and see. This strategy works well, except for one thing: we do not often verify our assumptions about what is really motivating the people we observe and interact with. We assume that what is real for ourselves is what is real for other people. At times, we are emotional two-year-olds who assume that what we make up to make sense of life is fact. Here is an example of what happens when we make up what is going on for another person.

Recently, Kelly had a conversation with her friend and colleague Dan about some struggles they were experiencing at work. A major reorganization had been implemented about four months before, and, as Dan said, "The tension in the office was so thick you could cut it with a knife." Kelly talked about her frustration over the limited amount of staff involvement in the reorganization planning process, and inadequate communication between management and staff to keep everyone up to date. They talked about the high-performance expectations being placed upon staff while the reorganization was under way. Dan focused on how angry he was that their manager, who had always been very approachable, had lately become totally unavailable. Dan told Kelly that he didn't know how much longer he could keep going under this pressure. With a chuckle in his voice, he said, "This madness is enough to drive a person to drink."

From Kelly's perspective, each of them had shared honestly about the issues that were shaping their experiences at work. She felt great at the end of the conversation because it seemed that she and Dan had gotten important issues off their chests and would be able to get through the difficulties together.

A few weeks later, Kelly learned that Dan was in a treatment center recovering from a relapse with alcoholism. Kelly knew that Dan was a recovering alcoholic, but because Dan chuckled when he talked about drinking, she thought his statement was just a passing expression. She wondered why Dan had not shared the seriousness of his struggle with her. When she and Dan talked later, he told Kelly that he was trying to share with her that he was having trouble managing stress and that he was scared that he was going to start drinking again. Hearing this, Kelly realized that because having more information about the reorganization was what helped her feel safe in the midst of uncertainty, she assumed Dan had the same need. Dan explained that he needed a sense of direct emotional support through this transition, which he was not getting from their boss or from Kelly. Kelly remembered hearing an edge in Dan's voice as he talked about his boss' unavailability, and wished that she had asked Dan to elaborate on that issue and how he might resolve it. During their conversation, Kelly had assumed that what was important to her was important to Dan. She made up the idea that his needs were the same as hers, and she had not thought to find out whether there was anything else going on with Dan.

When you listen to others but remain focused on your particular needs, you cannot clearly hear what is in their hearts. Everything you hear is distorted by your own issues. You miss out on rich moments to connect deeply with others. You miss opportunities to give support to others in ways that would be most helpful to them. This one point is critical: The world does not revolve around you. It revolves around all of us. The only way to feel listened to and heard is to give the gift of listening to others. Of course, there is no guarantee that everyone to whom you offer the gift of listening will return that gift. But it is almost guaranteed that you will not to be listened to by others if you do not give the gift of listening from your soul into someone else's.

THE NINETY-PERCENT RULE

A few years ago, I was facilitating a workshop when Charles, one of the participants, said to my cofacilitator Joan and me that we did not facilitate very well that day. Within seconds, several thoughts came to my mind. First, I became angry and said to myself, "Well, who does he think he is? Does he know who he's talking to? I'm a facilitator par excellence. And he's telling me that I didn't do a good job." Second, I thought, "Well, isn't this funny? I have just talked with the staff about the power of hot buttons today, and now I get to watch mine get hit." Then I thought, "I'd better be a good model for managing hot buttons. I'd better practice what I preach." Finally, I reminded myself, "Ninety percent of this is not about me. So find out what is going on with Charles right now and see how I can help."

While all of this rolled through my head, I watched it—like a sit-com about human nature—with a lot of internal laughter. Once I reconnected with the truth that most of Charles's issues were not about me, I was able to be present with Charles and really hear not only his words, but also the pain in his heart. The issues that the staff had discussed that day had been hard to explore. Charles and others wanted the facilitators to fix the issues quickly so that they didn't have to deal with their discomfort. Because Joan and I weren't doing that, Charles felt we weren't facilitating well. As I stayed emotionally present by remembering that Charles's issues were mostly about Charles, he and his colleagues began to feel safe enough to express their anxieties. As Charles and others were able to express their fears, the session was successful in facilitating the work they needed to do. It worked because I had applied the ninety-percent rule.

So what is the ninety-percent rule? Very simply: Ninety percent of what other people say or do in relation to you is not about you, but about themselves. This is true even if every sentence they say has your name in it, even if the examples they cite describe some of your less-than-glowing moments and illustrate areas in your life that need attention and healing.

Ninety is a somewhat arbitrary percentage. The purpose of using ninety percent is to emphasize that *most* of what the other person says is not about you. It is impossible and counterproductive to say precisely how much is attributable to whom. The "actual" percentage may vary from conversation to conversation, and will be based on factors, such as who the other individual is, the history of your relationship, and other issues in your lives at the time. The actual percentage is not important. What is important is to remember that you serve as a mirror for others, just as they do for you, and at times they may see and hear things in your behavior and your words that they don't like. Or something you say or do might push their hot buttons, which are based in unresolved past hurts. The ninety-percent rule is a tool that helps you avoid the emotional snags that impede listening and lead to communication breakdowns.

When you feel that you are getting caught in an emotional snag—like the one I was in when Charles said I didn't facilitate well—it might be helpful to repeat these words to yourself: "Ninety percent of this is not about me." Using the ninety-percent rule can keep you focused on the other person—both the content and emotion underlying what is said—and not your emotional response. The ninety-percent rule can help you listen to what the other person is really saying instead of what you might be making up or assuming. Applying the ninety-percent rule helps create enough emotional safety and healthy perspective that enable you to stay emotionally present with others.

The particular words and examples used by others in conversation are indicators of what may be going on inside them. When your emotional response gets caught in the mix, your ability to listen is minimized. If you soul listen you have greater ability to create a space that feels safe enough for others and yourself to begin to deal with what is really going on. This power is unleashed every time you or anyone applies the ninety-percent rule.

In response to hearing about this rule, a workshop participant once asked me why the rule is only ninety percent, instead of one hundred percent. She asked, "Isn't *everything* other people say really about them?" The answer is no, for two reasons—the temptation to overlook the emotional baggage you may be contributing and the pitfalls of creating emotional distance from others.

First, if I were to tell you that the things others say or do are one hundred percent about them, you might be tempted to separate yourself completely from the other person's issues and feelings. For many of us, when things become emotionally charged we want to say to the other person, "This is *your* problem. Why are you blaming it on me?" Sound familiar? Placing emotional distance between yourself and your conversation partner will likely lead to a breakdown in communication. It takes two people who are engaged and invested in the conversation for it to work well. Applying the ninety-percent rule helps you avoid divesting all of your interest in and commitment to the issue being discussed.

Second, the ninety-percent rule can serve as a reminder to you that there really may be something you have said or done, or perhaps something about the image you are projecting, that has triggered some uncomfortable feelings in the other person. For example, your husband has told you that you never believe him. It could be that the way you pointed your finger at your husband while you tried to emphasize an important point unconsciously reminded him of the schoolteacher who wrongly accused him of plagiarizing his school paper. Applying the ninety-percent rule, you are more likely to ask yourself, "What might I be doing or saying that could have triggered this emotional response in my husband?" With this question in mind, you will be better able to find out what is really going on in yourself and in your conversation partner. Perhaps there is something in your personality or approach to relationships that needs your loving and listening attention.

The ninety-percent rule does not suggest that you *caused* the other person to feel a certain way. Rather, it helps you explore what you may have said or done that triggered an emotional response in the other person. None of us has the power to cause someone to feel a certain way—angry, sad, happy. We can, however, help create emotional spaces in which others are more likely to respond in certain ways based on their fears, desires, and past experiences.

Of course, as I write this, several people pop into my head in whose presence I often experience anger. The anger that I experience is what I choose to feel in response to their words or behaviors. Often, my choice to feel angry is based on the limited information that I have at that time. For example, I was in a restaurant a few years ago and the server, Paul, was unpleasant, inattentive, and moved in slow motion. All of Paul's behaviors were irritating everyone at our table. Trying to salvage a fun dinner, I asked him how his day was going. At first, he said, "Okay." After a little probing, Paul then shared the struggles he was dealing with that day, and apologized for his poor service. After hearing what he was experiencing, my anger went away. It wasn't Paul who made me angry. I chose to be angry because I perceived that Paul did not value and respect me enough to provide better service. Once I had information that reminded me that ninety percent of Paul's actions were based on what was going on inside Paul and were not about me, then I chose not to be angry anymore. I still expected quality service, not because of my fear that I wasn't being valued and respected, but because I deserved it as a paying customer. And after he had the opportunity both to express his worries and to be heard, Paul provided much better service to our table.

I am not suggesting that it is the customer's responsibility to probe into the lives of workers who give poor quality service in order to get better service. The reality is that we all have a day at work or school or home when we may not be our most effective or pleasant. When you come across someone who is having such a day, you can choose how to handle the situation. You may choose to respond out of your own emotional baggage and perhaps help make the situation more unproductive, or you may apply the ninety-percent rule and help create a more loving and productive encounter. How you handle those encounters not only influences the rest of the day for the other person and yourself, but also touches each person you will come in contact with for the rest of the day and beyond because of the spirit we take with us from each encounter and pass on to the next. While we cannot cause anyone to feel what they feel, we can help create the conditions in which people are more likely to connect with certain feelings, based in either love or fear.

Soul listening involves remembering that not everything said by others is about us and that our responses are fully reflective of our issues and struggles. As we soul listen, how we interpret what we hear from others and ourselves frees us of the emotional worldview of the two-year-old within us. As we soul listen, we become more able to hear the Divine within our souls and recognize our connection with others.

REFLECTION ACTIVITIES

1. When you are in a stressful meeting at work or in an emotionally intense conversation at home, do you find yourself assuming that the other person's comments are about you? If so, how do you respond?

2. What are some of your past hurts or disappointments that have left tender emotional places in you?

3. How do you respond when someone touches on a subject that relates to your past hurts or disappointments?

4. Cite specific examples of times you felt so strongly about expressing your point that you talked more yet heard less. How did you feel as a result?

5. Recall one or two times that you felt that you and another person were really sharing and connecting, and later learned from the other person that she or he felt removed from what you were discussing. What was going on for you in the conversation that led you to believe true connection had happened?

6. What are some signals that might indicate you are so focused on your own issues that true connection with others is impeded?

7. Ask one or two loved ones—relatives or friends with whom you feel very safe and by whom you feel very respected—to help you watch for the signals that are focused solely on your issues. Discuss with them how you prefer for them to point out your signals to you.

NINE
FROM INNER CHATTER TO INNER PEACE

~

Knowing others is intelligence; knowing yourself is true wisdom.
Mastering others is strength; mastering yourself is power.
  —*Tao Te Ching*, No. 33

A s my poetry mentor, Leslie Shiel, says, "listening takes courage." It takes courage to listen to others and to listen within your own soul. As it relates to others, courage enables you to stay emotionally available to others, so that even if they say things you may not *want* to hear, you can hear from them what you *need* to hear. As it relates to yourself, courage enables you to ask critical questions about the hurts and fears that may be clouding your own ability to hear what is really being said. It takes courage, too, to be honest with yourself about what others reflect back to you about yourself and to use all interactions as opportunities to learn, grow, and heal.

We participate in two conversations simultaneously. One is the external, *inter*-personal conversation with our family members, friends, coworkers, clients, or strangers. The other is an internal, *inner*-personal conversation within ourselves. The external conversation is greatly influenced by the internal one. To be most effective as listeners, we must begin by soul listening to ourselves. This takes courage.

Inner-personal communication often consists of inner chatter that both distracts and distorts understanding. Inner chatter can be so loud that it impedes you from hearing clearly and being fully attentive to the interpersonal conversation.

We all experience inner chatter. Many of us are so accustomed to the noise of our inner chatter that often we do not recognize its presence. It can be like living near an airport, where although we become

~

desensitized to the frequent noise of airplanes, the sound neverthe-less influences how we listen and what we hear. We assume that we are listening clearly to others, yet what we hear is greatly distorted. Even when we are not consciously aware of it, our inner chatter largely determines the quality of our external listening and our over-all interpersonal communication. When the inner chatter is loud enough, it can completely block our ability to hear or totally distract our attention from what is being said.

In addition to making it hard to listen to others, inner chatter makes it hard to listen to yourself. It is like the experience of parents when they say to their noisy children, "I can't hear myself think," but the inner chatter comes from within. Inner chatter can be so loud and disruptive that it is difficult to identify your own feelings. Inner chatter makes it hard to distinguish between feelings about a current situation and feelings about similar situations in the past. Inner chat-ter can cause a listener's response to be based simultaneously on both the current experience and others from the past. This is not the same as using past experience to inform your understanding of the pres-ent—learning from history. Rather, this is an unconscious, emotional response that gets in the way of your full engagement with the pres-ent situation. Under such circumstances, both you and the person being listened to may begin to feel unsafe—you the listener because of the past associations creeping in, and the person being listened to in response to the listening style being demonstrated.

Here are a few indicators that inner chatter may be influencing how you listen and what you hear:

• the desire to blame someone else for the outcome of a situation or for the condition of your relationship

• dismissing or ignoring what the other person is saying without first considering any possible merits

• thinking, "I don't even need to listen to this; this is not my problem"

• recognizing your desire to start taking the other person's inventory; that is, focusing your attention on analyzing the emo-tional issues that the other may have that are the root cause of the situation

• wanting to end the conversation somewhat abruptly

• presuming that the other person is putting all of the blame on you

• feeling a physical sensation in your body (such as the heart/chest area, stomach, neck, back, or head) in response to something that has been said

• becoming unable to think or speak.

TAMING THE TRILOGY OF FEAR

Recognizing the presence of one or more of these indicators can help you deal with the presence of your own inner chatter. Each of these indicators is related to one or more of the fear responses, fight, flight, and freeze, discussed in chapter 5. There, our discussion of these three fear responses focused on the other person. You as a listener can also have fear responses. Inner chatter is often a reflection of fear, hurt, or other issues within you that stem from past experiences. The deeper your fear, the louder your inner chatter, and the harder it is for you to listen.

Inner chatter is your mind's way of protecting you. It represents the warning messages your mind sends to you when something in your conversation "makes" you feel unsafe. These warning messages—for example, "Don't trust him," "Remember what happened the last time," "She doesn't know what she talking about," "This doesn't make any sense"—often limit your ability to listen to and really hear others.

The self-protective wall of inner chatter resists penetration by the words, thoughts, and feelings of others, and even by your own attempts to overcome it. It limits the openness and vulnerability you need to soul listen effectively. Emotionally barricaded behind a force field of inner chatter, you are less able to foster safety in others. If you are feeling unsafe and inner chatter is influencing how you listen, your conversation will probably end in a listening shutdown. Here is an example.

Recently, seventeen-year-old Todd was attempting to tell his mother about some decisions he was trying to make regarding two girls he is interested in. He doesn't usually talk with his mother about the girls he dates, but he was feeling confused and stuck about what to do. Todd explained that one girl is very popular and all the guys think he is "the man" because he is dating her, but Todd has discovered that he doesn't have that much fun with her and that "she's all about herself." The other girl is in his chemistry class, she's very smart, already accepted at three great colleges. She is a teenage mother whose parents are going to take care of her baby while she's at school. The moment Christine heard Todd mention that the girl he really likes has a baby, her inner chatter took over: "Todd will never finish college if he gets involved with this girl. She's a loose girl and she's probably using sex to lure Todd. They're having sex. He's going to contract AIDS. He's going to get some sexually transmitted disease. Who else is he having sex with?" And so on. As Christine's inner chatter grew louder and louder, she heard nothing else that Todd had to say. She did not hear him explain how committed this girl is to completing her education and becoming a biochemist. She did not hear Todd tell her that they are not having sex. And Todd knew that he was not being heard. He stormed out of the room, committed to never discussing anything with his mother again.

Understandably, bells and whistles may ring loudly inside when we hear certain things from our children, spouses, and other loved ones, especially if we fear that they may make choices that we think are not in their best interest. Allowing the inner chatter to rule how we listen and respond, however, does not help them make good choices. Instead, it fosters an unsafe environment to which most people respond by fleeing as Todd did, fighting, or freezing. Following the voice of our inner chatter in such circumstances can lead us down paths opposite to those we seek.

SOUL LISTENING FOSTERS INNER PEACE

To foster a safe environment for communication, you must listen in a spirit of inner peace; that is, soul listen. To listen from your soul into the soul of another human being requires inner peace. Without it, all listening techniques have limited effectiveness. Having inner peace does not mean that you live a life with no fear, hurt, or anger. Rather, inner peace reflects a growing trust in the Divine, or God— even in the context of your fear, hurt, and anger—to provide the wisdom, strength, or material and other resources you need. In order to soul listen to others, you must first soul listen to yourself to understand and uncover your own fears. The soul-listening strategies that are applicable for fostering a greater sense of safety for others can also help you feel safe enough to tear through the self-protective wall created by your inner chatter.

There are a few strategies you can use to help quiet the chatter and to convert it to messages of healing. Some strategies relate specifically to certain listening styles, while others can be applied more broadly. Here are two important general strategies to begin transforming your inner chatter to inner peace.

First, ask yourself the question, "What am I afraid of, right now?" Exploring this question along with reflecting on the inner chatter indicators listed earlier helped me recognize that I had a lot more inner-personal dialogue going on than I could imagine. I discovered that most of my inner-personal dialogues were messages of fear, even though sometimes I was not certain what I was afraid of. Asking myself "What are you afraid of?" helped me draw information about my fears from below the surface. If my fears were about something very personal and close to my core beliefs, sometimes I would have to ask myself several times, "What are you afraid of?" When the answer came forth, I often knew of its truth because of the physical response I experienced upon recognition. For example, crying, having the sudden urge to sleep, feeling a sense of unburdening from my shoulders and back, or feeling an "Ah-ha!" sensation. Overall, the grip of the inexplicable fear no longer had its hold on me. As I listened into my soul to hear the truth of my fears, my inner chatter quieted and no longer had power over how I listened. Then I could begin to soul listen to myself and others.

Identifying and naming your own fears is vital to fostering a safe environment for yourself and others. Instead of being unconsciously directed by fears, you can speak empowering, life-giving, and healing messages to yourself. When you bring this kind of energy to your communication, it also enables you to engage with others in the same kind of spirit. This life-giving energy is a spirit of inner peace. Soul listening on the basis of such energy enables you to listen others' souls into life.

Let's use Christine and Todd's conversation as an example. If Christine had known about the indicators of inner chatter listed earlier, she might have recognized her pattern of dismissing everything Todd was saying without first considering any possible merits. If Christine had been able to recognize that her ability to listen to Todd was impeded by fear-based inner chatter, Christine might have been able to ask herself "What am I afraid of?" She might have then been able to articulate her fears: that Todd might not have the life Christine envisioned for him—college and material success; that she might be perceived as a failure as a mother; that her son might die. If Christine had acknowledged these fears, she might have been able to separate them from the issues that Todd needed to discuss. Getting in touch with her fears could have enabled Christine to listen to Todd's issues and discuss her concerns in a way that would not overshadow Todd's concerns or belittle his ability to make the right choices for his life. The end result might have been to expand the landscape of issues that Todd needs to consider in both the short and long term.

A second strategy, after you have begun identifying what you are afraid of, is to repeat, inwardly, a simple life-giving message that replaces the message of the inner chatter. Your mind thinks and processes information more quickly than you can speak, so your unconscious mind often sends messages to your conscious self while the other person is speaking. Although it is hard to stop the flow of thoughts, you can transform your inner chatter to inner peace by deciding what messages you choose to focus your thoughts on. Messages that are based in fear result in the clamor of inner chatter. However, messages that are life-giving and trust-building foster the inner peace needed to be emotionally present with others.

Again, let's look at Christine and Todd. What if, instead of making allegations about sexual promiscuity regarding the young woman that Todd likes, Christine developed a life-giving message like "With the right information, Todd makes good choices" or "Todd is seeking your advice, so listen to him" or "Todd is seeking your advice because he wants to make the right choices for his life." Infusing her mind with messages like these could have enabled Christine to stay emotionally present to Todd as he was seeking her help to solve problems. Quieting her inner chatter and being emotionally present to Todd could greatly enhance her ability to help her son make life-giving choices.

ANTIDOTES TO LETHAL LISTENING STYLES

In addition to its calming effect on the trilogy of fears, inner peace can help transform lethal listening into soul listening. Lethal listening styles reflect the inner chatter within your emotional or spiritual self. If your emotional self is filled with anxiety, or your spiritual self is in a state of unrest, you will experience even greater inner chatter when you attempt to listen. The transformation of inner chatter begins with a desire for such transformation, a desire that ultimately opens the door to soul listening.

Recall the lethal listening styles in chapter 4, and then read the following antidotes to those styles. As you explore the strategies below, you will note that breathing deeply is listed with each set of strategies. Because your breath is a physical manifestation of the Divine spirit within you, breathing can help you connect with the peace and wisdom of God. As you reflect on these strategies, look into your soul and ask which strategies can be most helpful for you, and then listen for guidance.

THE ANALYST ANTIDOTE

If you are an analyst, one who tends to analyze other people's lives, you may do this to distract yourself from looking at your own fears and struggles. Or your inclination might stem from your inner chatter messages saying you are inadequate, inferior, or bad; you analyze others as a way to prove to yourself how smart you are. To break the power of your inner chatter and move toward greater peace:

- look into your soul and ask why you need to share your analytical observations during the conversation
- explore what might happen if you do not share your thoughts
- remember that the person you seek to analyze is a mirror for you

- ask yourself if anything about your insights into the other person's life might be applicable to you
- invite the other person to share his thoughts and insights about his own issues first
- ask for permission before sharing your observations
- breathe deeply and feel the breath move through your body.

THE CO-OPTOR ANTIDOTE

The pattern of redirecting conversations to focus on your interests suggests the presence of a deep hunger for attention and love. Co-opting conversations from others cannot satisfy this hunger because, on some level, it does not feel like freely given love and attention. So the hunger continues. To minimize the likelihood of redirecting conversations inappropriately, in each conversation consider the following actions:

- remind yourself how you feel when someone redirects conversations away from your concerns
- ask yourself why you want to change the conversation
- ask yourself how the topic you want to introduce adds to the quality of the other person's life
- ask for permission before introducing a new topic
- ensure that you bring the conversation back to where it started
- invite the other person to share any other information or thoughts she may have
- remind yourself that taking attention from others cannot satisfy your hunger
- remember a time that you felt very loved by the other person or someone else, and bring that feeling into the present conversation
- create a mantra for yourself such as, "I am loved" or "There is enough love in the world for me"
- breathe deeply and feel the breath move through your body.

THE DRIFTER ANTIDOTE

A speaker or a topic might trigger your thoughts and emotional presence to drift away from a conversation, but neither of these can *cause* you to drift away. If you drift, you do so because of your own emotional state. Drifting occurs when you feel that something in your environment is not nurturing, or when anxiety about something else in your life looms over your current activity. You drift away when you are not staying in the present moment but focusing on something from the past or imagining something about the future. Your emotional self becomes separated from your physical self. Your body is present, but your mind is elsewhere. To avoid drifting away and remain emotionally present in the conversation:

- regard every human interaction as the potential for a divine communion
- remind yourself what it feels like to you when someone drifts away while you're speaking
- remind yourself of the sacredness of each listening moment as an opportunity to help water someone's soul more fully into life
- repeat or restate key words the other person has expressed
- ask questions to clarify meaning
- be aware of your own emotional or physical condition and how it may be influencing your ability to stay focused and, if helpful, share that information with the other person
- create a mantra for yourself such as, "This person and this moment are important to me; I will stay present to both"
- breathe deeply to keep your mind and body fully connected.

In addition, because drifting away may signal something about feelings within you, ask yourself: "Is there something about the content of the conversation that might be triggering an uncomfortable feeling within you?" For example, getting tired or bored may indicate your fear or anxiety. If there is some issue that you do not want to deal with in your own life, but which is brought closer to your emotional surface by what the speaker is sharing, you might disengage and drift off in order to avoid your own issues. Do a quick assessment of what may be going on inside you, listening to your body for signs as well. If the content is a source of anxiety, it may help to let the other person know, and to make a commitment to separate your feelings and issues from the speaker's.

Or ask yourself, "Is there something about the tone, pace, rhythm, or body language of the other person that makes it hard for you to stay present to the conversation?" For example, if you think very quickly and this person talks very slowly, it may be difficult to stay engaged. Perhaps asking the other person short questions or restating a few words very judiciously may help you stay present. I say judiciously because too much questioning or restating can feel intrusive to others.

THE INTERRUPTER ANTIDOTE

Frequent interruptions signal anxiety or a sense that something is lacking within the interrupter. Like co-optors, interrupters may feel a longing for more attention and interrupt in order to get it. A pattern of interruptions might also indicate an underlying anxiety and restlessness that limits the ability to stay focused on a single topic for an extended period of time. The anxiety or restlessness may in turn be indicating that the conversation's topic is stirring up thoughts and feelings the interrupter would rather avoid. To transform interruptive behavior:
- limit your interruptions to short, clarifying questions
- inform the other person that you have a related point to share when he is at a stopping point (he may ask you to share right away or later)
- ask yourself what might happen to you or the other person if your viewpoint is not heard in this moment
- look into your soul and ask if there is some issue you are avoiding or something that you are afraid of
- ask yourself how the content of your interruption complements what is being discussed
- ask for permission to interject and be prepared to accept no as the answer
- breathe deeply and feel the breath move through your body.

THE INTERROGATOR ANTIDOTE

Interrogators use questions to help them feel safe in their environment, and often do not disclose anything about themselves until they sense that they will not be taken advantage of. Asking all or most of the questions in a conversation signals that you are hiding from intimacy by minimizing the opportunity for others to get to know you. You collect lots of information about others, yet they know little about you. It is true that knowledge is power, and thus when you are an interrogating listener, you can have a sense of power. While you use this strategy to help yourself feel safe, you do so at the expense of the emotional safety of others.

You might contend that asking questions is your way of staying engaged and showing interest. Questions alone, however, will not accomplish that goal if the interrogation fosters a sense of unsafety within the other person and results in others disengaging from the conversation. Moreover, showing interest in the conversation is not the primary goal, but rather listening people into life, which calls for mutual sharing of questions and disclosures. To help create a sense of safety for yourself and others:

- be attentive to your own breathing between questions
- allow time for the speaker to answer one question and share something else before you ask another question
- invite the other person to ask any questions he may have
- disclose your tendency to ask a lot of questions and invite the other to let you know when she has had enough questions
- ask for permission before asking a series of questions
- breathe deeply and feel the breath move through your body.

THE KNOW-IT-ALL ANTIDOTE

Individuals who come across as know-it-alls are hampered from experiencing deep intimacy with others. People often take steps to protect themselves in the presence of know-it-alls or stay away from them altogether. The know-it-all approach to relationships is a way of exclaiming to the world, "Look how smart I am. I deserve to be loved," or "Look how smart I am. You can't hurt me." You might be thinking, "I'm just trying to be helpful." Your constant desire to be helpful is a statement about you. It might be driven by the belief that "If I help people, they will love me."

Like all of the other lethal listening styles, the know-it-all style emerges from a need to feel safe. But while it may foster a sense of safety for the listener, it does so at the expense of the emotional safety of others and at the expense of true intimacy. If you desire to transform your knowledge into information that is used to strengthen the sense of safety for you and others, consider these strategies:

- ask a few questions to learn from the speaker instead of telling what you know
- ask permission to share your knowledge
- look into your soul and ask yourself what you fear might happen if you do not share what you know
- say things to the other person such as, "I think I heard about that before, but tell me more from your experience"
- ask the other person how he felt or what he thought when he learned this information, and then share some of your feelings about the subject being discussed
- after the other person has discussed the issue to her satisfaction, offer to share something you recently learned that is related to the issue
- remind yourself that there is no competition or prize for being the smartest
- tell yourself, "I am loved regardless of my intellectual abilities" or "I deserve to be loved, period"
- breathe deeply and feel the breath move through your body.

THE OVEREXPLAINER ANTIDOTE

If you have ever explained something and then heard people say to you, "I *got* it" or "I'm not *that* stupid," you may have a tendency to overexplain. Overexplaining is a signal that you find your sense of self-worth in helping other people. As you seek to help, however, others often feel more frustrated than helped. Overexplaining, like knowing-it-all, indicates a desire to be recognized as smart, but often stems from deep insecurity. In the process of resolving their own insecurity, however, overexplainers often trigger others' insecurity about their intelligence. Because overexplaining signals a fear that you are not good enough to be loved without being helpful or smart, breaking the pattern of overexplaining begins as you grow in the knowledge that you are fully worthy of love.

To create new behaviors for listening and interacting, consider these actions:

- remind yourself that you are wonderful and loved
- ask yourself how much detail you would need to understand the information, and offer only that much detail, unless asked for more
- ask the other person, before you start to explain, what he already knows about the issue
- ask yourself why the explanation you intend to share may be important to the other person
- highlight the three or four most critical items rather than the entire list of key points
- keep track of how many times you explain the same point
- invite the other person to ask you questions and let those questions provide the basis for how much information you give
- tell yourself, "I am loved regardless of my intellectual abilities" or "I deserve to be loved, period"
- breathe deeply and feel the breath move through your body.

THE PESSIMIST ANTIDOTE

How you listen and respond reflects your beliefs about life. If you experience the world as one disappointment after the other, that belief is reflected in your conversations. You may even view the world pessimistically without realizing it. To get more information about your own worldview and beliefs, listen to how you respond to others and how you interpret what others say. If you notice that your interpretations are generally cynical, this is a signal that you view life pessimistically. What you might call being realistic, others might regard as pessimistic. Observe people's body language after you have responded to something they have just said. If they look away from you or change the subject quickly, it may suggest that your response was a pessimistic turn off for them. To rechannel your pessimistic listening style to a more life-giving and trusting approach:

- ask the other person to tell you more about what she likes regarding the information she has shared
- remind yourself that what the other person is saying is about him, not you

- look into your soul and ask for help in hearing and recognizing things in the conversation that are worthy of your trust
- tell the other person about something for which you are grateful that relates in any way to her
- ask yourself, "What am I afraid of?"
- immediately after the conversation, speak out loud three to five things that you enjoyed about the conversation you just had
- breathe deeply and feel the breath move through your body.

THE QUICK-FIXER ANTIDOTE

Although quick fixing is intended as a way to help others, at its heart it is often a strategy to deal with your own pain or fear about something. Quick-fixers cannot tolerate uncertainty or emotional discomfort—their own or that of others. The pain of others triggers emotional pain within quick-fixers. To quiet the pain of their conversation partner, quick-fixers come to the rescue with a barrage of suggestions to fix the situation. Quick-fixers project their own fear or pain onto other people and then doggedly strive to resolve the issues of the other. In so doing, they do not clearly hear what is important to others. Quick-fixing efforts might not be what others want or need. Being too intent upon fixing the situation may cause the listener to be less emotionally available and less helpful. To shift away from lethal quick-fixer behavior to soul listening, consider these actions:

- allow the other person to tell her whole story before you start offering suggestions
- ask if there are any primary issues, thoughts, or feelings the other person would like you to help him explore
- ask the other person what sort of support she would like in light of what she has shared
- ask for permission to share your comments and recommendations
- remind yourself, "This is her situation and she is capable of handling it" or "I can best be helpful by assisting him in getting the whole picture of what he needs"
- ask yourself, "What is being triggered in me?"
- breathe deeply and feel the breath move through your body.

THE SELF-PROTECTOR ANTIDOTE

Sometimes people need to vent before they are able to engage in the practical aspects of fact finding and problem solving. Their venting may feel like a personal attack, and it is easy for you as a listener to become very self-protective. Perhaps someone expresses an opinion about the school you attend, the business where you work, the religion you practice, or an idea you offered—you may begin to defend it and yourself without fully hearing their comments. Self-protection can be very passionate in nature. The process of self-protecting is usually characterized more by talking than by listening. When you move beyond maintaining healthy boundaries and self-respect and begin to engage in a defensive listening style, a listening shutdown often results, and the conversation dies.

If you find that your listening style is self-protective and conversations take place with raised voices or end abruptly without resolution, consider these actions:

- remind yourself that the other person's comments are an expression of her fears and concerns and are not designed to attack you
- allow the other person time to vent, repeating the words, "Ninety percent of this is not about me"
- imagine the other person as a child in danger, who because of frantic fear, is fighting against you, even though you are trying to help him
- look into your soul and ask for guidance about how to help the other person move through her fears in appropriate ways to the level of intimacy you and she can manage
- remind yourself that you are wonderful and loved, regardless of what the other person might say
- seek permission to ask questions or make comments to help the other person talk through his thoughts and feelings in a focused way
- breathe deeply and release anger out of your body through your hands. (Emotional and psychic energy flows into and out of your hands. To help you release feelings of anger, strongly shake your hands three to four times. This might sound strange to you, but try it; it works.)

Your use of various lethal listening styles will likely depend upon the circumstances of the conversation—that is, who the other person is, where the conversation is occurring, what other issues are going on in your life—and what issues are triggered for you and so on. Regardless of your lethal listening style, these strategies can help you move into a greater experience of inner peace.

Use your breath to help you become more grounded and calm. Breathing deeply, asking yourself, "What am I afraid of?" and replacing your inner chatter with life-giving messages are actions that can lead to greater peace, even when you are only talking with yourself. Inner peace can be not only a tool for soul listening, but a way of being. Replacing your inner chatter with life-giving messages helps you connect more deeply and fully with the Divine spirit within you.

REFLECTION ACTIVITIES

1. In your journal or in the back of this book, write what you want your relationships—at home, at work, with family and friends—to be, look, and feel like.

2. In what ways does your inner chatter hinder the experience of your relationships?

3. Listen closely to your inner chatter for four or five days. At least twice a day, write down specific issues addressed by your inner chatter. Later, review your notes and identify any specific themes in the chatter. What might these themes signify?

4. Develop simple statements, or mantras, to use as replacements for the messages of your inner chatter. It is important to memorize them when you are calm so that they automatically activate in emotionally loaded circumstances.

5. Set aside at least fifteen minutes each day for one week to be still and listen to your soul. What is your soul saying to you about which of your relationships can be strengthened, and how? Why do these specific relationships, and not others, have the potential to be strengthened?

TEN
REVIVING DYING COMMUNICATION

~

Then Jesus, deeply moved, came to the tomb. . . . Martha, the sister of the dead man, said to him, "Lord, already there is a stench because he has been dead four days." Jesus said to her, "Did I not tell you that if you believed, you would see the glory of God?" And Jesus looked upward and said, "Father-Mother, I thank you for having heard me. I knew that you always hear me. . . ." When he had said this, Jesus cried out with a loud voice, "Lazarus, come out!" The one that was dead came out.
—John 11:38-44, Christian Bible

We have looked at various ways to avoid listening shutdown through establishing safe environments for listening, and by laying the groundwork for listening as holy action. The strategies we have discussed are useful either at the beginning of conversations or during them. There are also some strategies that can be used in cases where communication has completely broken down.

Perhaps you have been in a conversation or even a relationship that you saw was dying and felt that there was nothing that you could do about it. And then, it was dead. You ask yourself: Is there something I could I have done differently?" But then you resign yourself to the thought that it is too late. You decide to bury your hopes and dreams for what the relationship could have been. Yet by using soul listening, there may be hope for new life in seemingly dead relationships. They need an infusion of the life-giving energy of God's spirit.

Some spirit-infusion strategies can be drawn directly from the story of Lazarus, quoted above. The Lazarus story provides some important insights into the choices many of us make when listening shuts down and communication seems to die. Even when communication has been pronounced dead, possibilities may remain for new life and restoration. To resurrect communication requires deep listening into your own soul.

~

First, the Lazarus story depicts the role of fear in our tendency to entomb the relationships we have given up on. After Lazarus died and was buried in a cave, a large stone was placed at the mouth of the cave to seal him in. Understandably, Martha, one of Lazarus's sisters, urged Jesus not to have the stone removed because she was convinced that the smell of decay would overpower them. The thought of that is enough to make most of us urge that the stone remain in place. Like Martha, we do not expect what we have lost can be restored, especially if the communication or the relationship has been dead for a period of time. We, too, fear that we will be overwhelmed by the stench of what has died. We wish not to be reminded of the factors that led to this death: broken promises, failure to forgive, hatred, and unhealed emotional wounds. We believe that dealing with the stench of these things might be more that we can bear. It is understandable to think, "Why subject myself to this stench? Life cannot return to this situation." So we choose not to deal with the stench. Yet this story illustrates that even if the stench is strong, the possibility that life can emerge from the tombs of frustration and despair makes it worth risking the stench.

Second, the Lazarus story demonstrates the vital role listening plays in the renewal process. Jesus takes the role of soul listener in this story, searching for guidance and trusting the Divine within his soul. Jesus begins by thanking God for hearing him. He knows that as God hears his request, the restoration of Lazarus to new life is possible. Jesus listens to God for the right moment in which to call Lazarus forth from the tomb. As a result, even in his state of death and decay, Lazarus hears Jesus' call to life. Jesus' call to life is infused with his confidence in the power of the Divine to work through him. Because Jesus listens, Lazarus, who has been pronounced dead, has the capacity to hear and respond to this call. The soul listening modeled by Jesus demonstrates that listening to and trusting the Divine within ourselves can create possibilities of life within others. As we soul listen, we create the conditions in which others can hear the call of God within them.

Third, the story captures the trust in the possibility of miraculous outcomes that are available when we seek wisdom and help from the Divine. Jesus did not give up, despite apparently hopeless circumstances and the unbelief of Lazarus's sisters. Jesus prayed for help. He prayed, not by asking or pleading, but by thanking God for hearing the prayer he spoke within his soul. His thanksgiving to God was an expression of Jesus' belief in the power of God to restore and revive even when all hope seems lost. Jesus models the power available to us when we seek and listen to Divine guidance with gratitude. As we are grateful and expectant for God to give us the wisdom we need, we become attuned to and participate in the activity of God that revives people's souls into life.

As this story shows, it is possible for communications and relationships to be restored, revived, and renewed. When resuscitation of communication is needed, soul listening requires, more than ever, humility, courage, and trust. It takes humility to admit that a conversation or relationship is in fact dead, and that wisdom and power beyond our own is needed to restore it. It demands courage to venture into unknown emotional and spiritual places within your soul where fears about what you might discover and uncover may abound. Efforts to revitalize a conversation are greatly strengthened when you believe that resurrection is possible. To revive dead communications calls for trust in God to give you the wisdom to know how to resurrect your communication. Listening into your soul for the leading of the Divine begins the process of restoring life. Go within your soul to seek and listen for help from God.

Scared to Death, Revived to Life

Looking back at communications and relationships that have died, we are likely to see some clues about how to restore those communications. Before the conversations died, your conversation partners probably provided information about their fears and how they respond to them. Soul listening with inner peace can enable you, in hindsight, to recall the information you have been given and how to use it to revitalize the conversation.

In chapters 5 and 9, we discussed the kinds of actions you might take to help others feel safe during conversations and avoid listening breakdown. This same information can be useful to you if a conversation has already died. Because fear causes communication to die, understanding the fear responses also can be very useful in resurrecting the communication. Below are some specific revival strategies related to each of the three fear response—fight, flight, and freeze.

FOUGHT-TO-DEATH

Depending upon personality, family background, and culture, the look of fighting in a conversation can vary tremendously. For some people, simply giving that certain "look" is equivalent to fighting words. For others, no fight is taking place unless lots of expletives are used. Others would say they are fighting only when the interaction becomes physical. We also vary our fighting tactics based on the circumstances. For example, those who use cursing as a fighting tool with family or friends might not do so with work colleagues. Regardless of the fighting tools used, it is important to know how to revive interactions that have died because of the fight response to fear. In chapter 6, coworkers Karla and Bill fought in the workplace in very indirect, covert ways as their company's sales continued to plummet. In chapter 5, spouses Doug and Kim fought by yelling and constantly interrupting each other. Let's look more closely at Doug and Kim.

After ten minutes of yelling over the phone, Kim hung up, outraged with Doug. Her inner chatter was urging her to call him back and tell him to stay at his mother's house that night and the rest of the week. She did not want to see him. She felt that this was the second time that day that she was cheated out of celebrating her promotion. She was just mad. Then she started wondering where he had been all afternoon. Was he really working or had he been out with some other woman? Her next barrage of thoughts centered on his comment about if it had been her mother, she would have returned the call immediately. This hurt her and made her angry. She thought, "How cruel of him to say something like that; he knows that I would give anything to have my mother still alive. Do I want to be married to a man who would make such a cruel statement to hurt me like that?" And so her inner chatter continued.

Meanwhile, inner chatter was racing through Doug's mind as well. He thought about the conversation that he and Kim had the previous weekend about starting a family. He wondered how good a mother Kim would be if her job would keep her from getting to their child in an emergency. He wondered if she would forget to call back the babysitter or nursery school. He worried that if his mother fell again and needed to come live with them, Kim would resent his mother and him.

Then his mother, having heard Doug and Kim yelling on the phone, simply said to him, "Doug, you know that Kim loves me very much, and she loves you. I never thought I would hear you talk like that to anyone, especially not to someone you love. Douglas, you owe her a huge apology." Doug stayed at his mother's house for two days, under the guise of caring for her. He did not talk with Kim that entire time. After the first day of sitting in his anger and fear, he remembered his mother's words about Kim's love for his mother and him. He knew that what his mother was saying was true. He was also reminded of how much he loves Kim and that he would not be happy without her as his spouse. He also thought about some of the hurtful things Kim said to him, and then he remembered some of the cruel things he had said to her. He reminded himself that their love was so strong they could make it through this hurtful situation. He knew that he had to apologize and try to correct his mistake. He prayed for guidance about how to restore their broken relationship. After making sure that his mother was okay, he went home.

When he arrived home, he began his apology by singing to Kim from outside. He made up a song that would not make it to the top of the charts, but because of the honesty and humility of his song, it was effective in reaching Kim's heart. By the time Doug entered their home, Kim and Doug were both ready to listen and be more vulnerable with one another. They were able to express their genuine regret for the things that they said to one another and to explore ways of not talking to each other in that way when they become scared or angry again.

Death-from-Flight

Some of us are not inclined to fight; rather, we flee from communication that does not feel safe and respectful. Such was the case with Todd in chapter 9, when he attempted to talk with his mother, Christine, about the girls he was dating. Because Christine reacted by verbally attacking Todd after hearing that one of these seventeen-year-old girls has a baby, Todd fled the scene. He went to a friend's house and did not return for several hours.

While Todd was gone, Christine began her process of listening into her own soul. She realized that she had to do something different in order to help her son make choices that were right for him and to keep the communication open between them. She used the time apart from Todd to ask herself what she was afraid of and she learned more than she could have imagined. First, she recognized that she was thinking about her own sister, who had become pregnant in high school. Christine's sister never finished high school, has been married two times, has children by three different men, and is now a single mother working in low-wage jobs. Christine feared that her son's life would be ruined if he connected with a girl like her own sister. Also, Christine volunteers in a hospice for women and men in the terminal stages of AIDS. Immediately she began to fear that if Todd were sexually active he would have a greater chance of being infected with the AIDS virus. All of these and many other thoughts raced through her mind. But after running through all these thoughts, Christine also reviewed what she knows about Todd: he is sincere, mature, and very committed to going to college and pursuing a profession.

When Todd returned home he did not want to speak to his mother. He went directly to his room, closed the door, and played loud music—a direct message to Christine that he did not want to speak to her. To respect his space and to foster a greater sense of safety for him, Christine wrote a note and slipped it under his door: "I'm sorry that I didn't listen to you. I really want to hear what you are thinking. I'll just listen when you're ready." Christine did not know how much more time Todd would need to feel safe enough to try talking again. She knew that she could not control that. Her only job was to offer to listen in a way that would express her love and respect for Todd. After a few days of avoiding his mother, Todd came to her and said, "Okay. Let's try again. But Mom, just listen this time. If you don't, that's it." Christine agreed.

FROZEN-TO-DEATH

When someone feels so unsafe that he or she can no longer think clearly enough to talk, the conversation freezes to death. This is what happened in chapter 5 with Jimmy and Kirk. When their phone conversation ended, with Kirk frozen and Jimmy fleeing, neither one felt safe enough to do anything but hang up the phone.

Kirk knew that if he told Jimmy that he had decided to ask someone else to be his best man, Jimmy would be extremely hurt and angry. During their conversation, Kirk was surprised to discover that being best man was so important for Jimmy. Discovering this, Kirk was at a loss for words. He was confused about how to resolve this in a way that would not hurt Jimmy. Kirk's inner chatter started flashing mental pictures of Jimmy getting drunk, creating a scene, and ruining the wedding because he was not the best man. He imagined Jimmy trying to make a toast at the wedding reception and shattering champagne glasses everywhere. Then he imagined Jimmy falling into the wedding cake. And so on and so on. With all this inner chatter, he was unable to separate his fears about Jimmy from his memories of his own drunken father. Because of the memories of his father, Kirk forgot that Jimmy has been sober for more than five years, and Kirk was unable to think clearly enough to know what to say or do.

Meanwhile Jimmy, in response to his fear, listened to his inner chatter telling him that Kirk no longer wanted him as a friend. His inner chatter scolded him, telling him to stop being a chump, a weakling, by begging to be Kirk's best man. Jimmy's inner messages got louder and louder, telling him that Kirk thought that he was not good enough for his new life. His inner chatter exclaimed, "Don't stay around and let Kirk kick you to the curb. You better let Kirk know that you don't need him. After all, you don't need him or his high-society wife. They are not your kind of people, anyway. They are plastic, phony people. You don't need him."

It worked well for Kirk that Jimmy needed to flee because ending the conversation gave Kirk the time and emotional space he needed to unfreeze. He needed a brief time alone so that he could think calmly, and begin a process of soul listening. Kirk remembered that Jimmy was sober now and, unlike Kirk's father, never became socially inappropriate even before he quit drinking. Kirk was then able to identify his fear of having any of his old buddies in the wedding, and to acknowledge that Jimmy would not do anything to sabotage Kirk and Patricia's wedding or marriage. Away from the noise of the conversation, Kirk was finally able to hear how important it was to Jimmy to be the best man. He was able to reconnect with his love for Jimmy. Kirk decided that he would ask Jimmy to be the best man.

After a time of quiet, Kirk called Jimmy said, "Jimmy, of course I want you to be my best man. You know you're my partner from way back. When you called me, I had so many thoughts going on that I couldn't even think straight. You know how it is getting married again. I don't even know what day it is sometimes. But two things I know: Even though I'm nervous about getting married again, I love Patricia. And I know that you're my main man. Will you be my best man?" Jimmy, after some hesitation, agreed.

REENGAGING AFTER THE DEATH

Because fighters express feelings, although not necessarily about the actual issue at hand, they are generally able to continue to dialogue after a relatively short time away. Conversations that are resumed with brief periods of light humor are great points of reentry for fighters.

Those who flee often need the most time away because all of their feelings are still locked inside and unexpressed. Yet even during this away time, those who flee benefit from being given gentle messages that you are there and able to listen when they are ready.

Freezers need quiet more than anything else. They can become overstimulated by the conversation and really need time to settle before beginning to think clearly again. The more quiet the space, the less time it takes for freezers to be able to be mentally and emotionally present again.

If you are a fighter, remind yourself of a funny time you had with the person with whom you are angry. Or think of something else that brings laughter and joy to you in order to help you revive your sense of connection with him.

If you are a person who flees, give yourself the distance you need as quickly as possible. The sooner you are able to get to a safe space, the less time away you will need. While you are away, imagine yourself in a warm protective embrace or brilliant light. It may help to have a particular face in mind, your concept of God, or no one, just the idea of comforting arms holding you.

If you are someone who responds by freezing, remind yourself, at a time that you are not experiencing a freeze reaction, that you need very quiet space (visually as well as aurally). Allow this message to get deep into your mind and body, conditioning yourself to go on automatic pilot when you are not able to think clearly about what you need.

Whether you fight, flee, or freeze, time and quiet space are needed to begin feeling safe enough for communication resurrection to occur. Regardless of the fear response, all people need assurances of love and respect in order to hear the call of the Divine to a new experience of life.

Breathing new life into dead communication is possible if you believe it is possible and if you soul listen first into your own soul, then into the souls of others. Listening into the soul brings forth the possibilities of new life, healing, and love. Listen deeply enough and you can hear the sounds of hope and life stirring within your soul. Begin restoring health to your inner-personal dialogue; then, through interpersonal communication, you can help listen a person's soul into new life.

Reflection Activities

1. Listen to your breath. Listen to your heartbeat. These are sounds of the life-giving power of the Divine. Practice breathing deeply as you begin each conversation to ensure that your mind and body are connected.

2. Think about a recent experience in which communication broke down and died. Ask within your soul what issues were present for you. Also ask for insight about issues that may have been present for the other person. What fear response did you use? What fear response did the other person use? What were the clues?

3. Think of a dead conversation that has been revived. What helped resurrect it? What did you do? What did the other person do? Was there any intervention from a third party? If so, how did that contribute to revitalize the dead communication?

4. Is there a communication or relationship in any area of your life that appears to be dead and that you are afraid to attempt resurrecting? If so, what are you afraid of? What will help you release the fear and strive for greater wholeness?

AFTERWORD

~

Each connection we make with another human being is a starting point, an
opportunity to love and learn, to grow in wisdom and, with practice,
expand the sphere of our love from that one relationship to many relation-
ships to the One all-inclusive, all-encompassing Relationship that is God.
—Khephra Burns and Susan L. Taylor, *Confirmation*

The premise of this book has been that listening is a holy activity that fosters the experience of divine life within others. Soul
listening is a blend of communication strategies and spiritual activity
that are both inner-personal and interpersonal. When listening is
engaged in only as communication, much of the potential richness
for each interaction is untapped and lost. When listening is
approached as a spiritual practice, both listeners and those being listened to can experience genuine connections grounded in respect
and love. When both the inner-personal and interpersonal dynamics
of listening are understood, we are able to connect with others
beyond mere listening. We go deeper, to the level of soul listening.
As these connections occur, growth and transformation are possible
in our homes, workplaces, and communities.

Soul listening has a ripple effect of passing love and respect to
people who are beyond the scope of the original conversations. Each
time we value someone by listening deeply, that individual is more
likely to value and listen to another person, who then passes that
sense of honor on to others. People become more likely to listen to,
smile at, and to offer help and loving challenge to others because one
person took the time to soul listen to them. Each time we soul listen,
we model for others how listening can bring forth the best in people.
We also model the ways in which we ourselves desire to be listened
to and valued. Through the ripple effect of listening we can transform the world. One person's action—especially holy action like listening—can create a positive difference in the lives of many.

~

Thank you for listening to the stories spoken from the pages of this book. I pray that you have gained some tools to carry with you into your own life stories. Thank you for your courage to listen.

NOTES

NOTES

Notes

NOTES

NOTES

NOTES

NOTES

OTHER RESOURCES FROM AUGSBURG

A Prayerbook for Husbands and Wives
by Ruthanne and Walter Wangerin, Jr.
128 pages, 0-8066-4062-6

A rich collection of read-aloud prayers for all occasions
that will draw husbands and wives closer, to God and to
each other.

A Prayerbook for Spiritual Friends
by Madeleine L'Engle and Luci Shaw
96 pages, 0-8066-3892-3

A collection of read-aloud prayers for friends. This book
will draw friends closer, to God and to each other.

How to Keep a Spiritual Journal
by Ron Klug
144 pages, 0-8066-4357-9

An indispensable guide that shows new ways to care for your
soul with prayer, spiritual readings, and journal exercises. This
book will help you understand your spiritual journey.

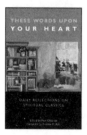

These Words upon Your Heart
edited by Paul Ofstedal
160 pages, 0-8066-4421-4

Arranged for daily reading, this collection provides thought-
provoking wisdom and guidance for the spiritual journey.
Ideal for individual reflection, the meditations can be used at
retreats, Bible studies, or other gatherings.

Available wherever books are sold.
To order these books directly, contact:
1-800-328-4648 • www.augsburgbooks.com
Augsburg Fortress, Publishers
P.O. Box 1209, Minneapolis, MN 55440-1209